THE PATH OF COMPASSION

ACKNOWLEDGMENTS

We gratefully thank the following copyright holders for permission to reprint essays: The Office of Tibet, for "Hope for the Future," by H. H. the Dalai Lama, reprinted from News-Tibet; Sulak Sivaraksa, for excerpt from Siamese Resurgence and A Buddhist Vision for Renewing Society; Jack Kornfield, for "The Path of Compassion," reprinted from The Esalen Institute Catalog, May-October 1983; Rochester Zen Center, for "Please Call Me by My True Names," by Thich Nhat Hanh, reprinted from Zen Bow; Diamond Sangha, for "To Enter the Marketplace," by Nelson Foster, reprinted from Blind Donkey and Kahawai; Buddhist Peace Fellowship-U.K., for Buddhism and Social Action, by Ken Jones; North Point Press, for "Gandhi, Dogen and Deep Ecology," by Robert Aitken, reprinted from The Mind of Clover; Rafe Martin for "Thoughts on the Jatakas," reprinted from The Hungry Tigress and Other Traditional Asian Tales; Grove Press, for "The Social Teachings of the Buddha," by Walpola Rahula, reprinted from What the Buddha Taught; Lindisfarne Association, for "The Edicts of Asoka," by Robert A. F. Thurman, excerpted from Lindisfarne Letter 8; The Eastern Buddhist Society, for "Nagarjuna's Guidelines for Buddhist Social Activism," by Robert A. F. Thurman, excerpted from The Eastern Buddhist, Spring 1983; Zen Center of Los Angeles, for "In Indra's Net," by Joanna Macy, which first appeared as an interview by Andrew Cooper in Ten Directions; Dharma Foundation, for "Interactivity," by Christopher Titmuss, portions of which first appeared as an interview by Joanna Macy in Inquiring Mind, Spring 1984; Minnesota Zen Meditation Center, for "Rape," by Judith Ragir; and the Fellowship of Reconciliation, for "Taking Heart," by Joanna Macy, reprinted from Fellowship, July 1982. A number of these essays first appeared in the Buddhist Peace Fellowship Newsletter: "Nurturing Compassion," by Christina Feldman; "In the Crucible," by Fred Eppsteiner; and portions of "Interactivity," by Christopher Titmuss, which were part of an interview by Joe Gorin and Ruth Klein.

THE PATH OF COMPASSION

Writings on Socially Engaged Buddhism

Edited by Fred Eppsteiner

A Buddhist Peace Fellowship Book
Revised Second Edition

PARALLAX PRESS
BERKELEY, CALIFORNIA

Printed in the United States of America

Co-published by Parallax Press and the Buddhist Peace Fellowship.

Cover design by Barbara Pope. Cover Photograph: Kuan Yin Bodhisattva, China, Northern Sung, c. 1025, wood, from the collection and courtesy of Honolulu Academy of Arts. Text layout adapted from a design by Barbara Pope. Composed in Altsys Goudy Old Style, using Microsoft Word on a Macintosh computer, by Parallax Press. Thanks to Dennis Maloney and White Pine Press for editorial assistance.

The Buddhist Peace Fellowship is a network of individuals and chapters formed to explore Buddhist approaches to peacemaking. For further information, please write to Buddhist Peace Fellowship, P.O. Box 4650, Berkeley, CA 94704. Parallax Press publishes books and tapes on mindful awareness and social responsibility. For a free catalogue, please write to Parallax Press, P.O. Box 7355, Berkeley, CA 94707.

Library of Congress Cataloging in Publication Data

The Path of compassion

    Includes bibliographical references.
    1. Buddhism—Social aspects.   2. Compassion (Buddhism)
I. Eppsteiner, Fred.
BQ4570.S6P37 1988   294.3378 88-9832
ISBN-0-938077-02-3

Contents

EXEMPLARS OF ENGAGED BUDDHISM

Editor's Preface

Increasingly over the past three decades, Americans have shown an interest in Buddhism. Bookstore shelves are filled with works on Buddhist philosophy, psychology, and techniques of mind training. Buddhist teachers roam the land, and in many cities and towns Buddhist centers are well established. The practice of meditation, which seemed quite mysterious just 25 years ago, is now widely accepted as a legitimate means to harmonious living.

Yet, despite this maturation and the acceptance of Buddhism and meditation even in the mainstream of society, our understanding of "the Way" is still incomplete. No one would disagree that the "inner" teachings and practices which lead to self-transformation and emancipation are at the core of Buddhism. But if the insights and awareness these practices help develop are not applied throughout daily life—to our work, our relationships, and our responses to crises near at hand and around the globe—then "selflessness" is a euphemism for selfishness, and detachment an excuse for indifference

In Western scholarship since Weber, there has been an implicit (and sometimes explicit) understanding that Buddhism shuns the worldly arena. For many practitioners, the teaching "just sitting [in meditation] is enough" has meant that it is not necessary to be aware when standing or walking, or even when hearing the cries of the world.

Recently there has been a significant shift in the recognition of Buddhism's social dimension. During the past two years, Buddhist groups have sponsored conferences on "Peacemaking: How to Be It, How to Do It," "Integrating Meditation & Social Action," "Buddhism and Nonviolence," and similar topics. The Buddhist Peace Fellowship's membership has tripled, three new Buddhist peace groups (two founded by academics) and a Buddhist AIDS Project have formed, and American Buddhist groups have begun offering hospice training, shelters for the homeless, and other significant projects for peace and the protection of all beings and the environment.

At this ripe time, we are happy to offer a new edition of *The Path of Compassion: Writings on Socially Engaged Buddhism.* It is our hope that this volume will offer inspiration and insight to all who have entered "The Path of Compassion" and will encourage further scholarship in the field of "engaged Buddhism."

May all beings be happy and free from suffering and realize peace and equanimity in their everyday lives.

Fred Eppsteiner
Naples, Florida
May 1988

KENNETH KRAFT

Engaged Buddhism: An Introduction

In the mid-1960s, as the war in Vietnam escalated, a group of Vietnamese Buddhist monks and nuns began working in a non-violent and nonpartisan way to aid their suffering countrymen. One spring day a team of eighteen Buddhists attempted to evacuate about 200 civilians trapped in a combat zone. A participant described what happened:

> The idea was to form two lines of Buddhist monks and nuns in yellow robes and lead the civilians out of the war zone. They asked me to carry a big Buddhist flag so that combatants of both sides would not shoot at us.... H. and a nun were quite seriously wounded by stray bullets. The trip lasted terribly long, as we had to stop many times, lying down on the streets and waiting for the shooting to lessen before continuing. We left the district early in the morning, but arrived in Pleiku only after dark. And what a bad time for arrival! It was time for the rockets. Pleiku was shelled. Unfortunately, we were very close to a military camp, and one rocket fell upon us, wounding seven of us. Children and women cried very much. We asked everyone to lie down and tried our best to help those who had been struck by the rocket.
>
> The most wonderful thing that happened that day is that we went through both Saigon and NLF soldiers but none of us was shot at. I must say that they were very thoughtful and kind. Had we not car-

ried the Buddhist symbol I do not know what would have happened. It seemed that as soon as they saw and recognized us, they immediately showed their respect for life.[1]

On that day and on many others, Vietnamese Buddhists parted the red sea of blood that was flooding their land. They displayed the equanimity, the courage, and the selflessness of true peacemakers. Remarkably, the writer of this account even expressed gratitude toward the soldiers on both sides. Rather than feeling rage or outrage, he saw the soldiers as thoughtful and kind, acknowledging them for their ability to respect life even in the midst of war.

The term "engaged Buddhism" refers to this kind of active involvement by Buddhists in society and its problems. Participants in this nascent movement seek to actualize Buddhism's traditional ideals of wisdom and compassion in today's world. In times of war or intense hostility they will place themselves between the factions, literally or figuratively, like the yellow-robed volunteers on the road to Pleiku. An American Zen teacher recently enumerated part of the new agenda:

> A major task for Buddhism in the West, it seems to me, is to ally itself with religious and other concerned organizations to forestall the potential catastrophes facing the human race: nuclear holocaust, irreversible pollution of the world's environment, and the continuing large-scale destruction of non-renewable resources. We also need to lend our physical and moral support to those who are fighting hunger, poverty, and oppression everywhere in the world.[2]

Because Buddhism has been seen as passive, otherworldly, or escapist, an "engaged Buddhism" may initially appear to be a self-contradiction. Isn't one of the distinguishing features of Buddhism its focus on the solitary quest for enlightenment? The contributors to this volume reply that no enlightenment can be complete as long as others remain trapped in delusion, that genuine wisdom is manifested in compassionate action. When they re-examine Buddhism's 2,500-year-old heritage, these authors find that the principles and even some of the techniques of an engaged Buddhism have been latent in the tradition since the time of its founder. Qualities that were inhibited in pre-modern Asian settings, they argue, can now be actualized through Buddhism's exposure to the West, where ethical sensitivity, social activism, and egalitarianism are emphasized. Believing that Buddhism may have unique resources to offer the West and the world, these writers do not hesitate to apply ancient Buddhist insights to actual contemporary problems. Thus Robert Thurman reads the Buddhist philosopher Nagarjuna, active in the second century C.E., "as if he were addressing us today."

The diversity of this anthology reflects the diversity of the emergent movement itself. Represented here are men and women from Tibet, Vietnam, Cambodia, Thailand, Sri Lanka, England, America, and other countries. Distinguished religious leaders share these pages with monks and nuns, laymen and laywomen, scholars, students, senior practitioners, and relative newcomers. The essays themselves are equally varied in background and style, drawn from the pamphlets, talks, and letters of an ongoing dialogue. The writers borrow from each other without diminishing the distinctiveness of their voices.

Though the writers' approaches to Buddhism may vary and their political perspectives may differ, there is consistency in the concerns that are addressed and the questions asked. The touchstone for engaged Buddhists is a vision of interdependence, in which the universe is experienced as an organic whole, every 'part' affecting every other 'part.' As Joanna Macy writes, "Everything is interdependent and mutually conditioning—each thought, word, and act, and all beings, too, in the web of life." Though classic formulations of this concept push the mind beyond conventional thought, the interconnectedness of things is also evident through ordinary observation. "One sees again and again," says Christopher Titmuss, "the way the mind influences the body, the body influences the mind, the way one influences the world, and the world influences one." On an international level, the interdependence of nations is equally apparent—a

Chernobyl meltdown contaminates Polish milk; a Philippine revolution ignites efforts for democratic reform in Korea. In such a world not even the most powerful of nations can solve its problems single-handedly.

For these thinkers, awareness of interconnectedness fosters a sense of universal responsibility. The Dalai Lama, exiled leader of Tibet, states that because the individual and society are interdependent, one's behavior as an individual is inseparable from one's behavior as a participant in society. The darker side of this realization is that each of us contributes in some measure to violence and oppression. The brighter side is that once we recognize our involvement in the conditions we deplore, we become empowered to do something about them. As the Vietnamese Zen teacher Thich Nhat Hanh writes:

> We need such a person to inspire us with calm confidence, to tell us what to do. Who is that person? The Mahayana Buddhist sutras tell us that you are that person. If you are yourself, if you are your best, then you are that person. Only with such a person—calm, lucid, aware—will our situation improve.

Because personal peace is connected with world peace on a fundamental level, we cannot meaningfully 'work for peace' as long as we feel upset, angry, or confrontational. "Nonviolence is a day-to-day experience," says Titmuss. The frenzied pace of life in technologically advanced societies exacerbates a tendency to cut oneself off from people and things. That separation is a kind of small-scale violence which breeds violence on a larger scale. Nhat Hanh notes, for example, how rarely we linger over a cup of tea with calm awareness; usually we gulp it down automatically, distracted by conversation, reading, music, or wandering thoughts. We thereby do violence to the tea, to the moment, and to ourselves. This linkage of personal and world peace is one of Buddhism's fresh contributions to politics.

Consistent with Nhat Hanh's gentle way of drinking tea, these essays reflect a spirit of tolerance and humility rarely encountered among partisans for a cause. A set of precepts developed by the Vietnamese Buddhists begins with three injunctions: avoid dogmatism, remain open, and do not force your views on others. The first reads:

> Do not be idolatrous about or bound to any doctrine, theory, or ideology, even Buddhist ones. Buddhist systems of thought are guiding means; they are not absolute truth.

Accordingly, these writers do not present Buddhism as an infallible system that holds all the answers to the problems we face. In the realm of socio-economic policy, they are willing to take points from a variety of other systems and faiths.

Nor is any conversion to Buddhism required. The ideas and practices offered here are assumed to be effective whether or not a Buddhist label is attached to them. "As part of our planetary heritage," writes Macy, "they belong to us all." Thurman's essay shows that Nagarjuna viewed all belief systems, Buddhist and non-Buddhist alike, as illnesses to be cured. "It does not matter what symbols or ideologies provide the umbrella," Thurman explains, "as long as the function is liberation and enlightenment."

Some of these accounts are deeply moving. Cao Ngoc Phuong, a Vietnamese nun, addresses a tender and meditative 'letter' to Chi Mai, a sister nun who deliberately gave her life to further the cause of peace. Though this act inspired many people, Phuong openly expresses her grief and the grief of Chi Mai's parents and friends. Another woman in a very different situation, an American in Minnesota, tells how her Buddhist practice helped her cope with the trauma of being a rape victim. In fact, personal exposure to unusual suffering is a thread that links many of the contributors. The Cambodians, Tibetans, and Vietnamese have seen their compatriots slaughtered, their countries occupied, and their traditional cultures dismantled. There is an undercurrent of sadness in this book, a sorrow that recognizes the current pain of the world and contemplates the terrible pain that would accompany a nuclear or an ecological disaster.

Yet engaged Buddhists refuse to turn away from suffering or sadness. They believe that no one is really able to avoid feeling pain for what is happening in the world today, try as one might to keep such feelings from coming to consciousness. For centuries Buddhism has focused on suffering as the starting-point of the religious life. Mahayana Buddhism teaches that nirvana is present *within* samsara; that is, awakening or salvation are not separate from suffering and its causes. Engaged Buddhists are updating this mysterious alchemy by transmuting despair into empowerment. Thus the rape victim reports, even amidst her lingering fear: "I actually was able to convert this catastrophe into an effective tool for my personal and spiritual growth."

In typical Buddhist fashion, this book is not content simply with doctrine and theory. Buddhism has always emphasized that the spiritual path is a way that is "walked not talked." Scattered throughout this volume are practical insights and specific techniques that one can apply oneself. If you have a hot temper, says the Dalai Lama, try timing the duration of your anger, making each bout a minute or two shorter than the last. Macy offers guided meditations adapted from traditional Buddhist sources on such themes as death, compassion, empowerment, and mutual trust. For example, the media bombard us continually with evidence of the suffering of fellow beings, but before we can get in touch with our feelings of sadness, empathy, or distress, we are hit with the next alarming image or fact (or distracted by a commercial). Macy suggests that such moments are an opportunity to put down the newspaper, turn down the radio or the TV, and focus on breathing:

> Breathe in that pain like a dark stream.... let it pass through your heart.... surrender it for now to the healing resources of life's vast web.... By breathing through the bad news, rather than bracing ourselves against it, we can let it strengthen our sense of belonging in the larger web of being.

Recently, Buddhists have been seen taking action in widely varying contexts around the globe, sometimes nonviolently and sometimes violently. In certain cases their behavior has been deplored by sensitive observers, and troubling issues have surfaced.

In the essays that follow, the reader will find Buddhist arguments that condone armed defense of one's homeland, as well as Gary Snyder's support for such means as "civil disobedience, outspoken criticism, protest, pacifism, voluntary poverty, and even gentle violence if it comes to a matter of restraining some impetuous crazy."

Other Buddhists might insist that if the collective karma of a nation is to be invaded, even destroyed, then violent resistance would only create further karmic burdens. There is an incident in the Buddhist scriptures in which Shakyamuni Buddha, after failing twice to turn back an invader nonviolently, stands aside and allows his clan to be massacred.[3] There is also a Jataka story, cited here, in which the Buddha in a former incarnation sacrifices himself for a starving tigress unable to feed her cubs. Are our only options violent self-defense or genocidal self-sacrifice?

Because the implications of an engaged Buddhism have not yet been explored in a profound and systematic way within the Buddhist tradition, issues like these remain unresolved. To mention some further questions that have arisen: Are ancient Buddhist teachings adulterated or trivialized when linked to specific social goals? What does it mean to present release from suffering in terms of literacy, irrigation, or marketing cooperatives? What are the actual roots of nonviolence in Buddhism? Does 'Buddhist nonviolence' differ in any meaningful way from the nonviolence of other traditions? Can Buddhism offer any guidance in our handling of social organization, economics, or technology? Many formerly Buddhist nations are now under the sway of communism; can some form of Buddhism and some form of communism co-exist or even support each other? While several of these questions are addressed in this collection, there is a consensus that further inquiry, reflection, and discussion must follow.

"Compassion" is a pleasant-sounding word, newly fashionable in American campaign rhetoric. As a political buzzword, it implies a rejection of attitudes or policies associated with recent constraints on social services. The compassion valued by Buddhists is something different—a deep sense of oneness with all beings, a spontaneous impulse born of suffering. As the yellow-robed Buddhists of Vietnam demonstrated, at times the "path of compassion" may even be strafed with bullets. Yet it is also as ordinary as a smile of greeting, as close as the hand that offers help. In simple terms, "The philosophy is kindness."

NOTES

[1] Letter to Cao Phuong, May 1972, quoted in *Zen Bow* (Rochester: The Zen Center), 5:5, Winter 1973, p. 11.

[2] Philip Kapleau, *A Pilgrimage to the Buddhist Temples and Caves of China* (Rochester: The Zen Center, 1983), p. 26.

[3] *Ekottaragama*; Hajime Nakamura, "Violence and Nonviolence in Buddhism," in Philip P. Wiener and John Fisher, eds. *Violence and Aggression in the History of Ideas* (New Brunswick: Rutgers University Press, 1974), p. 176.

MAHA GHOSANANDA

Invocation: A Cambodian Prayer

For more than a decade, the people of Cambodia have known the great suffering of warfare, persecution, and famine. I pray that like millions of peaceful Khmer people, all people will find strength and compassion in their hearts and guidance in these words of the Buddha:

> In those who harbor thoughts of blame and vengeance towards others, hatred will never cease. In those who do not harbor such thoughts, hatred will surely cease.
>
> For hatred is never appeased by hatred. It is appeased by love. This is an eternal law. Just as a mother would protect her only child, even at the risk of her own life, even so let one cultivate a boundless heart towards all beings. Let one's thoughts of boundless love pervade the whole world above, below, and across, without any obstruction, without any hatred, without any enmity. Whether one stands, walks, sits, or lies down, as long as one is awake, one should maintain this mindfulness. This, they say, is to attain the blessed state in this very life.[1]

May all beings exist in happiness and peace. Then there is no problem!

The suffering of Cambodia has been deep.
From this suffering comes great compassion.
Great compassion makes a peaceful heart.
A peaceful heart makes a peaceful person.
A peaceful person makes a peaceful family.
A peaceful family makes a peaceful community.
A peaceful community makes a peaceful nation.
A peaceful nation makes a peaceful world.
Amen.

---

[1]*Metta Sutta*

Thoughts on Spiritual Practice
and Social Action

Hope for the Future

I want to speak with you about the importance of kindness and compassion. When I speak about this, I regard myself not as a Buddhist, not as the Dalai Lama, not even as a Tibetan, but as one human being, and I hope that you will think of yourself as a human being rather than just an American, or a Westerner, or a member of a particular group. These things are secondary. If you and I interact as human beings, we can reach this basic level. If I say, "I am a monk; I am a Buddhist," these are, in comparison to my nature as a human being, temporary. To be human is basic. Once you are born as a human being, that cannot change until your death. Other characteristics—whether you are educated or uneducated, rich or poor—are secondary.

Today we face many problems. Some are essentially created by ourselves, based on divisions due to ideology, religion, race, economic status, and other factors. Because of this, the time has come for us to think on a deeper level, on the human being level, and from that level to respect and appreciate the sameness of ourselves and others as human beings. We must build closer relationships of mutual trust, understanding, respect, and help, regardless of differences in culture, philosophy, religion, or faith.

After all, all human beings are made of flesh, bones, and blood, wanting happiness, and not wanting suffering. We all

3

have an equal right to be happy, and it is important to realize our sameness as human beings. We all belong to one human family. We quarrel with each other, but that is due to secondary reasons, and all of this arguing, cheating and suppressing each other is of no use.

Unfortunately, for many centuries, human beings have used all sorts of methods to suppress and hurt one another. Terrible things have been done. We have caused more problems, more suffering, and more mistrust, and created more hatred and more divisions.

Today the world is becoming smaller and smaller. Economically and from many other viewpoints, the different areas of the world are becoming closer and much more interdependent. Because of this, international summits often take place; problems in one remote place are connected with global crises. The situation itself expresses the fact that it is now necessary to think more on a human level rather than on the basis of the matters which divide us. Therefore, I am speaking to you as just a human being, and I earnestly hope that you are also reading with the thought, "I am a human being, and I am here reading the words of another human being."

All of us want happiness. In cities, on farms, even in remote villages, everyone is quite busy. What is the purpose? Everyone is trying to create happiness. To do so is right. However, it is very important to follow a correct method in seeking happiness. Too much involvement with superficialities will not solve the larger problems.

There are all about us many crises, many fears. Through highly developed science and technology, we have reached a very advanced level of material progress, both useful and necessary. Yet if you compare the external progress with our internal progress, it is quite clear that our internal progress is falls short. In many countries, crises—terrorism, murders, and so on—are chronic. People complain about the decline in morality and the rise in criminal activity. Although in external matters we are highly developed and continue to progress, at the same time we neglect our inner development.

In ancient times, if there was war, the effect was limited. To-day, because of external material progress, the potential for de-struction is beyond imagination. When I visited Hiroshima, though I knew something about the nuclear explosion there, I found it very difficult to see it with my own eyes and to meet with people who actually suffered at the moment of the bombing. I was deeply moved. A terrible weapon was used. Though we might regard someone as an enemy, on a deeper level an enemy is also a human being, also wants happiness, also has the right to be happy. Looking at Hiroshima and thinking about this, at that moment I became even more convinced that anger and hatred cannot solve problems.

Anger cannot be overcome by anger. If a person shows anger to you and you respond with anger, the result is a disaster. In contrast, if you control anger and show the opposite attitude—compassion, tolerance, patience—then not only do you yourself remain in peace, but the other person's anger will gradually di-minish. World problems also cannot be challenged by anger or hatred. They must be faced with compassion, love, and true kindness. Even with all the terrible weapons we have, the weapons themselves cannot start a war. The button to trigger them is under a human finger, which moves by thought, not un-der its own power. The responsibility rests in thought.

If you look deeply into such things, the blueprint is found within—in the mind—out of which actions come. Thus, first controlling the mind is very important. I am not talking about controlling the mind in the sense of deep meditation, but rather in the sense of cultivating less anger, more respect for others' rights, more concern for other people, more clear realization of the sameness of human beings. Take the Western view of the Eastern bloc—for instance, of the Soviet Union. You must look at the Soviet Union as brothers and sisters; the people of Russia are the same as yourselves. From the Russian side, they should also look on your side as brothers and sisters. This attitude may not solve problems immediately, but we have to try. We have to begin promoting this understanding through magazines and through television. Rather than just advertising to make money for ourselves, we need to use these media for something more meaning-ful, more seriously directed towards the welfare of humankind. Not money alone. Money is necessary, but the actual purpose of money is for human beings. Sometimes we forget human beings and become concerned just about money. This is illogical.

After all, we all want happiness, and no one will disagree with the fact that with anger, peace is impossible. With kindness and love, peace of mind can be achieved. No one wants mental unrest, but because of ignorance, depression and so on, these things occur. Bad attitudes arise from the power of ignorance, not of their own accord.

Through anger we lose one of the best human qualities—the power of judgment. We have a good brain, allowing us to judge what is right and what is wrong, not only in terms of today's concerns, but considering ten, twenty, or even a hundred years into the future. Without any precognition, we can use our normal common sense to determine if something is right or wrong. We can decide that if we do such and such, it will lead to such and such an effect. However, once our mind is occupied by anger, we lose this power of judgment. Once lost, it is very sad—physically you are a human being but mentally you are not complete. Given that we have this physical human form, we must safeguard our mental capacity of judgment. For that, we cannot take out insur-ance. The insurance company is within ourselves: self-discipline, self-awareness, and clear realization of the shortcomings of anger and the positive effects of kindness. Thinking about this again and again, we can become convinced of it; and then with self-awareness, we can control the mind.

For instance, at present you may be a person who, due to small things, gets quickly and easily irritated. With clear understand-ing and awareness, that can be controlled. If you usually remain angry about ten minutes, try to reduce it to eight minutes. Next week make it five minutes and next month two minutes. Then make it zero. This is the way to develop and train our minds.

This is my feeling and also the sort of practice I myself do. It is quite clear that everyone needs peace of mind; the question is how to achieve it. Through anger we cannot. Through kindness, through love, through compassion, we can achieve peace of mind. The result will be a peaceful family—happiness between parents and children; fewer quarrels between husband and wife; no worries about divorce. Extended to the national level, this attitude can bring unity, harmony, and cooperation with genuine motivation. On the international level, mutual trust, mutual respect, and friendly and frank discussions can lead to joint efforts to solve world problems. All these are possible.

But first we must change within ourselves. Our national leaders try their best to solve our problems, but when one problem is solved, another crops up. Trying to solve that, there is another somewhere else. The time has come to try a different approach. Of course, it is very difficult to achieve a worldwide movement of peace of mind, but it is the only alternative. If there were an easier and more practical method, that would be better, but there is none. If through weapons we could achieve real, lasting peace, all right. Let all factories be turned into weapons factories. Spend every dollar for that, if that will achieve definite, lasting peace. But it is impossible.

Weapons do not remain stockpiled. Once a weapon is developed, sooner or later someone will use it. Someone might feel that if we do not use it, millions of dollars will be wasted, so somehow we should use it—drop a bomb to try it out. The result is that innocent people get killed. A friend told me that in Beirut there is a businessman who deals in weapons solely to make money. Because of him, many poor people in the streets get killed—ten or fifteen, or a hundred every day. This is due to lack of human understanding, lack of mutual respect and trust, not acting on a basis of kindness and love.

Therefore, although attempting to bring about peace through internal transformation is difficult, it is the only way to achieve a lasting world peace. Even if it is not achieved during my own lifetime, that is all right. More human beings will come—the next generation and the one after that—and progress can continue. I feel that despite the practical difficulties and the fact that this is regarded as an unrealistic view, it is worthwhile to make the attempt. So wherever I go, I express this, and I am encouraged that people from many different walks of life receive it well.

Each of us has responsibility for all humankind. It is time for us to think of other people as true brothers and sisters and to be concerned with their welfare, with lessening their suffering. Even if you cannot sacrifice your own benefit entirely, you should not forget the concerns of others. We should think more about the future and the benefit of all humanity.

If you try to subdue your selfish motives—anger, and so forth—and develop more kindness, more compassion for others, ultimately you will benefit more than you would otherwise. So sometimes I say that the wise selfish person should practice this way. Foolish selfish persons always think of themselves, and the results are negative. But a wise, selfish person thinks of others, helps others as much as he or she can, and receives good results.

This is my simple religion. There is no need for complicated philosophies, not even for temples. Our own brain, our own heart is our temple. The philosophy is kindness.

SULAK SIVARAKSA

Buddhism in a World of Change: Politics Must be Related to Religion

LIFE AND TEACHINGS OF THE BUDDHA

When Prince Siddhartha saw an old man, a sick man, a dead man, and a wandering monk, he was moved to seek salvation, and eventually he became the Buddha, the Awakened One. The suffering of the present day, such as that brought about at Bhopal and Chernobyl, should move many of us to think together and act together to overcome such death and destruction, to bring about the awakening of humankind.

The origin of Buddhism goes back to the sixth century B.C.E. The founder was an ordinary man, the prince of a small state in Northern India, now Nepal. He was deeply concerned about the problems of life and death and of suffering, and after much effort, he discovered a solution to these deepest of human problems. His solution was universal and radical. It addressed suffering as such, not just this or that sort of suffering. Neither the cause nor the cure of suffering were matters of revelation. The Buddha simply discovered them, as many others could have done before or since. He appeared as a doctor for the ills of humankind. Buddhist liberation—*nibbana*—is accessible to anyone at any time,

indifferent to caste or social standing. It requires neither the
mastery of an arcane doctrine nor an elaborate regimen of asceticism. In fact, the Buddha condemned extreme austerity, as
well as intellectual learning that does not directly address urgent
questions of life and death.

The Buddha's original teaching remains a common fund for
all branches of Buddhism, and it is expressed in the Four Noble
Truths: Suffering; the Cause of Suffering, namely desire or craving; the Cessation of Suffering; and the Way to do so, namely the
Eightfold Path. It is not enough merely to attain an intellectual
understanding of these propositions. We have to make them part
of our life. Like medicine, they must be taken. It does no good to
have aspirins in the bottle; they must be internalized. If we do not
regard suffering as something real and threatening, we do not
take the message of the Buddha seriously.

The Buddha found that birth is the cause of such suffering as
decay and death, and traced the chain back to ignorance. Then
he contemplated the way in which ignorance gives rise to
karmic formation, which in turn produces consciousness and so
on through the twelve-link chain of causation (paticcasamuppada),
until he came to birth as the cause of decay and death. Working
backward, he saw that cessation of birth is the cause of the cessation of suffering, and finally, he discovered that the cessation of
ignorance is the ultimate cause of cessation of the whole chain.
He is said to have become the Buddha by means of this
contemplation up and down the chain of causation. In other
words, he contemplated the way to deliverance from suffering
and found that the cause of suffering is ignorance and that by
extinguishing ignorance, suffering is extinguished.

The Buddha, having attained the peaceful state of nibbana, is
full of compassion. This attitude of compassion or benevolence
should be taken as the fundamental principle in our social life.
Compassion or love toward one's neighbors is highly esteemed in
Buddhism. Compassion is expressed in the Pali word metta,
which is derived from mitta (friend). Compassion therefore
means "true friendliness."

BUDDHISM IN SOCIETY

Buddhism enters the life of society through the presence of individuals who practice and bear witness to the Way, through their thought, speech, and actions. Anyone who looks at this world and society and sees its tremendous suffering, injustice, and danger, will agree on the necessity to do something, to act in order to change, in order to liberate people.

The presence of Buddhist sages—or indeed of any humanist leaders who have attained the Way—means the presence of wisdom, love, and peace. In most societies, the so-called leaders are themselves confused, engrossed in hatred, greed, or delusion, so they become the blind who lead the blind. When they do not have peace of mind, how can they lead others without love or compassion? In Buddhism, we believe that the presence of one such person is very important, and can have an important influence on society. In Buddhist terminology, we use the term "emptiness of action," or "non-action." To act in a way that arises from non-action is to act in a way that truly influences the situation in a nonviolent way. Naturally, humanists and masters of the Way contribute to the ends to save life, but their most valued contribution is their presence, not their actions. When they act, their actions are filled with the spirit of love, wisdom, and peace. Their actions are their presence, their mindfulness, their own personalities. This non-action, this awakened presence, is their most fundamental contribution.

Since the time of the Buddha there have been many meditation masters. They may appear not to be involved with society, but they contribute greatly. For me, they are the spring of fresh water, living proof that saints are still possible in this world. Without them, religion would be poorer, more shallow. These meditation masters, monks who spend their lives in the forests, are very very important for us and for society. Even those of us who are in society must return to these masters from time to time and look within. We must practice our meditation, our prayer, at least every morning or evening. In the crises of the present day, those of us who work in society, who confront power and injustice daily, often get beaten down and we become tired. At least once a year, we need to go to a retreat center to regain our spiritual strength, so we can return to confront society. Spiritual masters are like springs of fresh water. We who work in society need to carry that pure water to flood the banks, to fertilize the land and the trees, to be of use to the plants and animals, so that they can taste something fresh, and be revitalized. If we do not go back to the spring, our minds get polluted, just as water becomes polluted, and we are not of much use to the plants, the trees, or the earth.

Most of us who are in society must be careful, because we can become polluted very easily, particularly when confronted with so many problems. Sometimes we feel hatred, sometimes greed, sometimes we wish for more power, sometimes for wealth. We must be clear with ourselves that we do not need much wealth or power. It is easy, particularly as we get older, to want softer lives, to want recognition, to want to be on equal terms with those in power. But this is a great danger. Religion means deep commitment, and personal transformation. To be of help we must become more selfless and less selfish. To do this, we have to take more and more moral responsibility in society. This is the essence of religion, from ancient times right up to the present.

Many people, particularly in the West, think that Buddhism is only for deep meditation and personal transformation, that it has nothing to do with society. This is not true. Particularly in South and Southeast Asia, for many centuries Buddhism has been a great strength for society. Until recently, Buddhist values permeated Burma, Siam,[1] Laos, Cambodia, Sri Lanka, and other Buddhist countries. But things have changed, due mainly to colonialism, materialism, and western education. Many of us who were educated abroad look down on our own cultures, on our own religious values.

Society has become much more complex. Whether we like them or not, industrialization and urbanization have come in, and traditional Buddhism does not know how to cope with them. It did very well in rural, agrarian societies, but in urbanized societies, with the complexities of modern life, Buddhism does not know what to do. The Buddhist university in Siam, for example, is a place where monks read only the scriptures, study only the life of the Buddha in the traditional way. Meanwhile, Bangkok has become like New York or Chicago, but the monks are not aware. They think it is just a big Siamese village, as it was when I was born. They do not realize how complex Bangkok has become. Indeed the monks still have food offered to them in the traditional way, so why should they think things have changed?

They still feel that because we have a king, the government must be just, since the government supports the Sangha. This is the Dhammaraja, or "Wheel-Turning King" theory. But in reality the governments have been corrupt in Siam for at least 30 or 40 years. Most came to power through *coup d'états*, often violent. In the last *coup d'état*, several hundred people, mostly students, were killed, and several thousand were put in jail. Still, many of the monks feel that the governments are just, so it is the duty of those of us who have a certain spiritual strength and who can see what is going on to tell them that it is otherwise. This is the duty of any religious person. We have to build up political awareness. Politics must be related to religion.

We must also build up economic awareness. Economics also relates to religion. We need what E. F. Schumacher called Buddhist economics—not just western capitalistic economics, which is unethical and unjust, which only makes the rich richer and the poor poorer. Yes, we also need some socialist economics, but socialist economics makes the state too powerful. We really need Buddhist economics. If we are to be poor, we must be poor together, poor but generous, share our labor, share our thought, share our generosity. We need to build on that. So it is our duty to make economists aware of Buddhist economics.

In *Small Is Beautiful*, Schumacher reminds us that Western economists seek maximization of material gain as if that they hardly care for people. He says that in the Buddhist concept of economic development, we should avoid gigantism, especially of machines, which tend to control rather than to serve human beings. With gigantism, we are driven by an excessive greed in violating and raping nature. If bigness and greed can be avoided, the Middle Path of Buddhist development can be achieved, i.e. both the world of industry and agriculture can be converted into a meaningful habitat.[2] I agree with Schumacher that small is beautiful in the Buddhist concept of development, but what he did not stress is that cultivation must first come from within. In the Sinhalese experience, the Sarvodaya Shramadana movement applies Buddhism to the individual first. Through cultivated individuals a village is developed, then several villages, leading to the nation and the world.

Political awareness and economic awareness are related to ourselves and our society, and very much related to our own culture. To drink Coca Cola, to drink Pepsi Cola, for example, is a great mistake. It is not only junk food, it is exploiting our country economically. Both the Coca Cola Thailand Company and the Pepsi Cola Thailand Company have an ex-prime minister as president. This already makes us suspect something exploitative politically and economically. Culturally, the exploitation is insidious. Pepsi Cola and Coca Cola make the villagers feel ashamed to offer us rain water to drink. They feel they must offer us something in a bottle. And each bottle costs them one day of their earnings.

For another example, a multinational pineapple company recently expanded its empire into my country. They bought a lot of land from our farmers, who were very proud—poor but proud to be farmers. Now they have become landless. They do not grow rice any more, they just grow pineapples for that company. At first, the company bought at a very good price; later on, they lowered the price; still later on, the farmers just became their employees. In a country without labor unions, without the right to strike, the farmers are at the mercy of the pineapple company (which was started by a missionary).

THE TRUE SPIRIT OF BUDDHISM

Some Westerners want to become Buddhist monks only to escape from the world of turmoil, to benefit only themselves. My own experience over the past 30 years clearly indicates that Buddhism in the West has been practiced by many who did not want to get involved with society. However a new generation of Buddhists in England and America have displayed a robust feeling and an inclination to become involved in the spirit of Buddhism.

Phrakru Sakorn is a good example of what I mean by the spirit of Buddhism. He is a Thai monk in his 50's, the abbot of Wat Yokrabat in Samut Sakorn province, a provincial monk who only completed elementary education. Samut Sakorn is only one province away from Bangkok. The people there are mostly impoverished, illiterate farmers. The province is usually flooded with sea water, which perennially destroys the paddies, leaving the people with little or no other means of subsistence.

Most of the people had been driven to gambling, drinking, or playing the lottery. Being fully aware of the people's situation, Phrakru Sakorn decided to try to help the people before attempting to make any improvements in his own temple or spending a lot of time preaching Buddhist morals. Phrakru organized the people to work together to build dikes, canals, and to some extent, roads. He realized that poverty could not be eradicated unless new crops were introduced, since salt water was ruining the rice fields. He suggested coconut as a substitute, based on the example of a nearby province.

Once the people of Samut Sakorn started growing coconuts, Phrakru advised them not to sell them because middle men kept the price of coconuts very low. He encouraged them to make coconut sugar, using traditional techniques to do so. With the help of three nearby universities which were interested in the development and promotion of community projects, Phrakru received assistance, and the people of Samut Sakorn began selling their coconut sugar all over the country. He has since encouraged the growing of palm trees for building material, and the planting of herbs to be used as traditional medicine.

Before the end of the Vietnam War, I asked Ven. Thich Nhat Hanh whether he would rather have peace under the communist regime which would mean the end of Buddhism or rather the victory of the democratic Vietnam with the possibility of Buddhist revival, and his answer was to have peace at any price. He argued that Buddhism does not mean that we should sacrifice people's lives in order to preserve the Buddhist hierarchy, the pagodas, the monasteries, the scriptures, the rituals, and the tradition. When human lives are preserved and when human dignity and freedom are cultivated toward peace and lovingkindness, Buddhism can again be reborn in the hearts of men and women.

The presence of Buddhism in society does not mean having a lot of schools, hospitals, cultural institutions, or political parties run by Buddhists. It means that the schools, hospitals, cultural institutions, and political parties are permeated with and administered with humanism, love, tolerance, and enlightenment, characteristics which Buddhism attributes to an opening up, development, and formation of human nature. This is the true spirit of nonviolence.

Having grasped the spirit of Buddhism, we must face the world in full awareness of its condition. In Buddhist terminology, the world is full of *dukkha*, i.e. the dangers of impending world destruction through nuclear weapons, atomic fall-out, air, land, and sea pollution, population explosion, exploitation of fellow human beings, denial of basic human rights, and devastating famine. We must realize that if we wish to avoid these catastrophes, humanity must immediately stop all partisan brawls and concentrate all its abilities and energy in the urgent effort to save ourselves.

The struggles of the peoples in the Third World might go on for many more dozens of years. Because of wars, resources are wasted and economies cannot be built up. Third World governments want to spend more and more money to buy weapons from rich countries to fight civil wars, and they fall farther and farther behind on the path of development. The situation grows more and more complex. The fate of humanity is too great a burden. What can we do?

World *dukkha* is too immense for any country, people, or religion to solve. We can only save ourselves when all humanity recognizes that every problem on earth is our own personal problem and our own personal responsibility. This realization can only occur when the divisions and strife between religions, peoples, and nations cease. We can only serve ourselves when, for example, the rich feel that they should contribute towards alleviating the famine of the world. Unless the rich change their lifestyle considerably, there is no hope of solving this problem. Those in the northern hemisphere must see the difficulties in the Third World as their own problem. They must see the denial of basic human rights in Siam and Chile as their own problem, and the famine in Calcutta as their own agony.

The thoughts and spirit of Buddhism are well suited to the needs of a united world and to the removal of dividing, painful boundaries. The wisdom of Buddhism can provide a shining and illuminating outlook. The language of Buddhism must offer answers which fit our situation. Only then will Buddhism survive, today and tomorrow, as it has in the past, influencing humankind positively and generating love, peace, and nonviolence. The Buddha himself declared:

> All actions, by which one acquires merits are not worth the sixteenth part of friendliness (*metta*) which is the emancipation of mind; for friendliness radiates, shines and illumines, surpassing those actions as the emancipation of mind, just as all the lights of the stars are not worth the sixteenth part of the moonlight, for the moonlight, surpassing them all, radiates, shines, and illumines.[3]

In the whole of Buddhist history, there has never been a holy war. Surely Buddhist kings waged war against one another, and they might even have claimed to do so for the benefit of mankind or for the Buddhist religion, but they simply could not quote any saying of the Buddha to support them however just their war might have been. The Buddha said,

> Victory creates hatred. Defeat creates suffering. The wise ones desire neither victory nor defeat... Anger creates anger... He who kills will be killed. He who wins will be defeated... Revenge can only be overcome by abandoning revenge... The wise ones desire neither victory nor defeat.

There is much to be learned from the wisdom and compassion of the Buddha in this pluralistic world.

NOTES

[1] My country has become very Westernized, perhaps more than anywhere else in Southeast Asia. We even changed our name from Siam to Thailand. This kingdom was known as Siam until 1939 when it was changed to Thailand, and it remains so officially. It has been ruled by one dictator after another, and Bangkok has become a kind of second or third rate Western capital. There is not a single Buddhist value left in Bangkok, except as decoration for the tourists, or for mere religious ceremony, and Western urbanization is really beyond our grasp. To me the name Thailand signifies the crisis of traditional Siamese values. Removing from the nation the name it had carried all its life is the first step in the psychic dehumanization of its citizens, especially when its original name was replaced by a hybrid, Anglicized word. This new name also implies chauvinism and irredentism, and I refuse to use it. I prefer to use the name Siam.

[2] E. F. Schumacher, *Small is Beautiful* (London: Blond & Briggs, 1973).

[3] *Anguttara-nikaya.*

CHRISTINA FELDMAN

Nurturing Compassion

The Buddha was once asked by a leading disciple, "Would it be true to say that a part of our training is for the development of love and compassion?" The Buddha replied, "No, it would not be true to say this. It would be true to say that the whole of our training is for the development of love and compassion."

All the various expressions of religion and spirituality join in stressing the importance of nurturing love and compassion in the development of spirituality. Our own human experience supports the urgency and necessity for developing and actualizing love and comp____on. The mind which is disconnected from the heart la____ ____n of interconnectedness and lacks the power of inr____ ____. How often do we need to see our resolu-tior____ ____gress corrupt our society and rape our p____ ____sage that our minds need to be at-____ in a vision of connectedness if ____ in a life-enhancing rather ____nnot end the clinging, ____undermine the bal-____ structures of human ____s is not one that disregards the power and application of the mind, nor is it one that glorifies the heart to the exclusion of all else. It is a vision that appreciates the interconnectedness of our own hearts and minds and recognizes that we have the potential to actualize that rapport in a sensitive and intelligent relationship to life.

A spiritual mystic said, "Of what avail is an open eye, if the heart is blind?" What are the roles of our hearts, our feelings in our spiritual journey? Do they open as an effect of insight or are they qualities that need conscious nurturing, or both? Are they inferior or a secondary tool in spiritual growth or are they an integral and essential facet of mystical vision? We can agree that entering on a spiritual path does not mean that we place our feelings and hearts in storage. Self-understanding is an undeniable foundation of spiritual growth and this inner journey involves an intimate encounter with every aspect of our being. The impact of feeling and emotion is intensified, both the joy and the pain of our feelings are magnified in this encounter. There is rejoicing and there is anguish, heights of elation and depths of despair. Our hearts dance with lightness as we discover dimensions of peace and understanding within, they also grieve with sorrow as we discover the prisons we create for ourselves unknowingly through a lack of self-understanding and disharmony. This inner journey is marked by an enhanced and growing inner sensitivity, one that can listen to, accept, and grow through both the joy and the sorrow. We find ourselves forsaking the pursuit of personal perfection and also the denial of imperfection. To become someone different, to pursue a model of personal perfection is no longer the goal; nurturing our capacity to listen inwardly, to grow through the challenges of each moment, cherishing the freedom to be who we truly are without the distortions of our conditioning, brings spiritual richness. In that development of inner sensitivity, we discover that our capacity to feel and to respond is enhanced as our hearts open.

Sensitive inwardly, we can be sensitive in every moment of our lives, in every pore of our being. Learning to listen inwardly, we learn to listen to our world and to each other. We hear the pain of the alienated, the sick, the lonely, the angry, and we re-

joice in the happiness, the fulfillment, the peace of others. We
are touched deeply by the pain of our planet, equally touched by
the perfection of a bud unfolding. With our thoughts, our actions,
our lives, we treasure freedom and nurture it. We look to conflict
and suffering without fear, and nurture the ways to bring about its
end. Sensitivity brings an inner connection with the total range
of our dynamics and resources, our bodies, feelings, and mind.
Respect for the power and fertility of our heart is born, and we
truly appreciate the healing power of love, sensitivity, and compassion. We learn to respect the heart for its power to connect
us on a fundamental level with each other, with nature and with
all life. We learn to respect the power of love and compassion to
heal division, alienation, anger, and greed. We come to understand that our spirituality is made whole through founding itself
upon the heart, upon love and compassion. We cannot afford a
spirituality devoid of consciously nurturing love and compassion,
a spirituality divorced from the heart. The price we pay is imbal-
ance within, a world of brutality. Our mind articulates and cele-
brates our heart, our connection with love and compassion, our
inner rapport is reflected in sensitivity and respect for all life.

Detachment without wisdom deteriorates into passivity and
irresponsibility. Responsiveness is equated with reaction and
held with contempt. Spiritual invincibility is sought for and
equated not solely with outer withdrawal, but also with a
distancing from the responses of our own hearts. In this deterio-
ration we learn to measure the progress of our detachment by the
paralysis of our own responses. "We are in this world but not of
it" is a statement taken to extremes by absolving ourselves of responsible action and intervention in conflict in the name of detachment. If we witness an injustice, do we, in the name of detachment, simply walk past it? If we are exploited, harmed, or
undermined, is it a sign of spiritual development or holiness to
dissolve into meekness and humility, telling ourselves that surely
we are going to learn from this pain? How much pain are we
willing to accept in our lives in the name of being enriched by it,
justifying our passivity in the name of developing humility and
selflessness? How many times must we be injured unnecessarily,

undermined and dismissed before we can listen to our hearts and truly understand that we have learned all that is going to be learned and that our selflessness is only the disguise of fear, and perpetuates exploitation?

Once, in a monastery in the East, temporarily relegated the role of rice cleaner and dust chaser, I had the virtues of my part praised by a visiting monk. He spoke of his envy for me in having this marvelous opportunity to develop humility and selflessness through serving him. My questioning of his unwillingness to exchange roles became only evidence in his eyes of my failure to benefit from this "marvelous opportunity." Discriminating wisdom is the capacity and willingness to refuse to perpetuate or participate in any form or expression of exploitation, oppression, or action that perpetuates suffering, division, and conflict. It is the wisdom that is equally dedicated to supporting and nurturing ways of being that are life enhancing.

There is a tendency in spiritual teaching and in the practice of spirituality to focus upon and emphasize the unwholesome, the imperfections within that deny liberation. Seeing the apparently bottomless depths of personal imperfection, the path to liberation seems to call for concerted efforts to transcend, overcome, and renounce these endless imperfections. It can seem almost sacrilegious to seek for joy, lightness, and celebration in the midst of so much misery. Self-punishment, asceticism, and denial appear to be the appropriate responses to our impure state of being. No one would deny that renunciation and transcendence are essential ingredients of spiritual growth, but, whether the path of growth inherently needs to be a path of misery is an assumption we need to question. If our spiritual goal is personal perfection, then inherent in the path we adopt is the striving for self-improvement and betterment. We hold models and ideals, adopted or created, of personal perfection, and measure our progress and improvement by our capacity to equal our models. The presence of anything within ourselves that we deem an imperfection becomes a sign of failure, and the absence, no matter how temporary, of those imperfections, is greeted as a sign of success and progress. Lost within our measuring and judging of ourselves, we

fail to appreciate the degree to which our adopted path has become a path of rejection and pursuit, lacking in the qualities of
love and compassion. Our liberation and spiritual wholeness becomes endlessly postponed, sacrificed on the altar of impossible
personal perfection. Our humanness is distinguished not only by
its potential for realization and change, but also by its fallibility.
Ignoring the latter, we attempt to reduce spiritual insight to psychological triumph.

Joy, love, and compassion are essential ingredients in spiritual
growth. We are enriched by their nurturing, and our world is
enriched by their actualization. Profound joy is a celebration of
our vision of connectedness, a vision that dissolves division and
the myth of separation. We must let our hearts dance and rejoice
with love and compassion and yearn wholeheartedly for oneness
and for wholeness. Opening our hearts, we celebrate a love that
can embrace our pain, the pain of our world. Attuning ourselves
to sensitivity and gentleness, we can listen to the song of a bird,
feel the touch of the wind on our cheek, touch the heart of another person and connect with the fundamental rhythm of our
universe. Still within, the divisions and the conflicts are healed,
and we appreciate the uniqueness and preciousness of all life.
Insight is born of this stillness, a transforming vision of connectedness and oneness.

JACK KORNFIELD

The Path of Compassion:
Spiritual Practice and Social Action

How can we reconcile the question of service and responsibility in the world with the Buddhist concepts of non-attachment, emptiness of self, and non-self? First we must learn to distinguish love, compassion, and equanimity from what might be called their "near-enemies."

The near-enemy of love is attachment. It masquerades as love: "I love this person, I love this thing," which usually means, "I want to hold it, I want to keep it, I don't want to let it be." This is not love at all; it is attachment, and they are different. There is a big difference between love, which allows and honors and appreciates, and attachment, which grasps and holds and aims to possess.

The near-enemy of compassion is pity. Instead of feeling the openness of compassion, pity says, "Oh, that poor person! They're suffering; they're different from me," and this sets up separation and duality. "That is outside me. I want it. I need it to be complete." I and it are seen as different.

The near-enemy of equanimity is indifference. It feels very equanimous to say, "I don't give a damn, I don't care, I'm not really attached to it," and in a way it is a very peaceful feeling, a great

24

relief. Why is that? Because it is a withdrawal. It is a removal from world and from life. Can you see the difference? Equanimity, like love and compassion, is not a removal. It is being in the middle of the world and opening to it with balance, seeing the unity in things. Compassion is a sense of our shared suffering. Equanimity is a balanced engagement with life. The "near-ene-mies"—attachment, pity, and indifference—all are ways of back-ing away or removing ourselves from the things which cause fear. Meditation does not lead to a departure from the world. It leads to a deeper vision of it, one which is not self-centered, which moves from a dualistic way of viewing ("I and other") to a more spontaneous, whole, unified way.

Vimala Thakar has been a meditation teacher in India and Europe for many years. In many ways, she is a Dharma heir to Krishnamurti. After she had been working in rural development for many years, Krishnamurti asked her to begin to teach, and she became a powerful and much-loved meditation teacher. Then she returned to her rural development work, teaching meditation considerably less. I asked her, "Why did you go back to rural development and helping the hungry and homeless after teaching meditation?" and she was insulted by my question. She said, "Sir,"—as Krishnamurti does—"I am a lover of life, sir, and I make no distinction between serving people who are starving and have no dignity in their physical lives and serving people who are fearful and closed and have no dignity in their mental lives. There is no difference to me. I love all of life, and the way that I give is to respond to whatever is presented to me."

It was a wonderful response! There is a Sufi or Islamic phrase that puts it together. It says, "Praise Allah, and tie your camel to the post." It expresses both sides: pray, yes, but also make sure you do what is necessary in the world. It is what don Juan called "a balance between controlled folly and impeccability." Controlled folly means seeing that all of life is a show of light and sound and that this tiny blue-green planet hangs in space with millions and billions of stars and galaxies, and that people have only been here for one second of world-time compared with millions of years of other changes. This context helps us to laugh more often,

to enter into life with joy. The quality of impeccability entails realizing how precious life is, even though it is transient and
ephemeral, and how, in fact, each of our actions and words do
count, each affects all the beings around us in a very profound
way.

If I wanted, I could make a very convincing case for just practicing sitting meditation and doing nothing else; and an equally
convincing case for going out and serving the world. Looking at
it from the first side, does the world need more oil and energy
and food? Actually, no. There are enough resources for all of us.
There is starvation, poverty, and disease because of ignorance,
prejudice, and fear, because we hoard and create wars over
imaginary geographic boundaries and act as if one group of people is different from another. What the world needs is not more
oil, but more love and generosity, kindness and understanding.
Until those are attained, the other levels will never work. So you
really have to sit and meditate and get that understanding in
yourself first. Only when you have actually done it yourself can
you have the insight to effectively help change the greed in the
world and to love. Thus, it is not a privilege to meditate, but a
responsibility. I will not go any further with this argument, but it
is very convincing.

As for the other side, I only have to mention Cambodia or
Somalia and the starvation in Central Africa and India, where
the enormity of the suffering is beyond comprehension. In India
alone, 350 million people live in such poverty that they have to
work that day to get enough food to feed themselves that night,
when they are lucky. I once interviewed a man in Calcutta who
was 64 years old and pulled a rickshaw for a living. He had been
pulling it for 40 years, and he had ten people dependent on him
for income. He had gotten sick once the year before for ten days,
and after a week they ran out of money and had nothing to eat.
How can we let this happen? Forty deaths per minute from starvation in the world; $714,000 a minute spent on machines to kill
people. We must do something!

Both arguments are totally convincing. The question is how to
choose what to do, what path to take, where to put our life en-

ergy, even which spiritual path to follow. Spirituality in this country has blossomed and it is exquisite! It is also kind of confusing. There are so many ways to go—how to decide? How can we choose what to do this year, today? For me the answer has been to simply follow the heart. Sometimes it is clear that we must take time to meditate and simplify—to do our inner work. Sometimes it is clear that we must begin to act and give and serve.

I can just share my own experience, which is very immediate. Ordinarily I spend my year teaching meditation retreats. A couple of years ago, though, war began raging in Cambodia. I know the people there and a couple of the local languages, and something in me said, "I'm going," and I went, not for very long but long enough to be of some assistance. This year, feeling a real need to bring a greater marriage of service and formal meditation, I went to India again with some friends to collect tapes for radio and television on the relationship between spiritual practice and social responsibility. And now I am back teaching meditation.

I did not think about it much at the time. It just seemed that it had to be done, and I went and did it. It was something immediate and personal. The spiritual path does not hold out some simple solution, some easy formula for everyone to follow. It is not a question of imitation. You cannot be like Mother Teresa. She is Mother Teresa, and she is wonderful. Even if you tried, you wouldn't be like her. You have to be yourself. That means listening to your heart and knowing the right thing to do, and then doing it in the spirit of growing in awareness and service.

It is not always easy. Nobody said it was supposed to be. It is not even easy getting out of the womb. There is a lot that is hard in having a human birth. It is difficult, but it is also beautiful. There is a story about Mother Teresa and her ring. Someone said to Mother Teresa, "Well, you know, it's easier for you. You're not married or in a relationship." "What do you mean? I am married," she answered, holding up the ring that signifies a nun's marriage to Jesus, "and he can be very difficult, too!"

There are two great forces in this world. One is the force of killing. That is how dictators run countries. They run them by killing other people—by being willing and not being afraid to kill. But there is another great force that is equally powerful, maybe more so, and that is the force of not being afraid to die. That is the only force that is powerful enough to meet someone who is not afraid to kill. What Gandhi showed in India was the power of this force. Thousands of troops came from one direction to partition and to quell the riots, while from the other direction came one person, Gandhi, whose strategy eventually succeeded. How did he do it? He said, "I am going to starve. I won't eat until you stop the rioting and insanity." He knew that his people cared so much for him, they would not let him die. That is what love is—putting yourself on the line. The spirit of service, in little ways and big ways, is really what practice is: serving ourselves, serving the world around us. It is a giving of ourselves or a giving up of ourselves to the unity, the whole, and not just this little "I-me-mine." It is powerful and joyful, really wonderful to learn to give.

One of the exquisite experiences in my travels in India was to see the holy city of Benares on the Ganges River bank, covered with hundreds of temples and stores and markets. Along the Ganges there are bathing ghats, where people come to pay their respects and bathe as a purification, and there are also ghats where they bring bodies to burn. I had heard about them for years and had always thought, "Wow, that must be a heavy place. They bring bodies there and they burn them and it must be really intense." It was amazing to be rowed in this little boat down the Ganges in a very quiet way up to where there were twelve different fires going, and six or eight of them had bodies on them. Every half an hour or so, they would carry a new body down to the fires, chanting, "Rama Nama Satya Hei," which could be translated as "The only truth is the name of God." Yet it was not heavy at all. It was peaceful and quiet and sane. It was really sane. It was just, "Well, that is what happens."

What does this have to do with meditation practice? It has to do with the recognition that, in the face of the tremendous suffering of the world, there can be joy that comes not from denying pain and seeking pleasure, but from our ability to sit in meditation, even when it is difficult, and to let our hearts open to our experience. It is really the nitty-gritty work of practice to sit here and feel your sadness and my sadness and our fear, our desperation and our restlessness, to open to them and begin to learn that to love is to die to how we wanted it to be, and to open more to its truth. To love is to accept. It is not a weakness. It is the most extraordinary power.

There is a beautiful sutra that talks about the blessings of those who grow in this kind of love. It is called the *Cultivation of Lovingkindness*, and it lists 50 blessings that come through diligent practice. It says that if your heart is open and loving, you will have sweet dreams and fall asleep more easily, and awaken contented, with a smile. The *devas* and angels will love and protect you. Men and women will love you, and weapons will not be able to harm you. Guns will misfire, and poison won't work, and things that come to harm you will not be able to, it is such a powerful force. People will welcome you everywhere into their countries and into their homes, and you will have pleasant thoughts, and your mind will become very quiet. Animals will sense this love, and they will love you back. Elephants will bow to you. Your voice will become sweet and soft, and your babies will be happy in the womb and happy when they grow up. If you fall off a cliff, it says, a tree will always be there to catch you. Your countenance will be serene, your eyes shiny, and you will become awakened.

Even though this is what the sutra says will happen, we don't talk about lovingkindness early on in our retreats. People are sitting with restlessness and anger and knee pains, not joy, peace, or serenity. But I will tell you a secret, what is really important in the practice: true love is really the same as awareness. They are identical. Not the near-enemies of "I want" or "I'm in love with," but deeper love than that. True love is to see the divine goodness, the Buddha nature, the truth of each moment, and to say, "Yes," to allow ourselves to open, to accept. That is our practice every moment, whether in sitting meditation or action-meditation, whether sitting on a cushion or sitting near the barricades in protest. It is to be aware, to see the truth which frees us. It is opening to what is now, to what is here, and to seeing it as it is.

The forces of injustice in the world loom so huge, and sometimes we feel so tiny. How are we to have an impact? I will leave you with the words of don Jose in Castaneda's *Tales of Power*: "Only if one loves this earth with unbending passion can one release one's sadness. A warrior is always joyful because his love is unalterable and his beloved, the earth, bestows upon him inconceivable gifts....Only the love for this splendorous being can give freedom to a warrior's spirit; and freedom is joy, efficiency, and abandon in the face of any odds."

THICH NHAT HANH

Please Call Me by My True Names

I have a poem for you. This poem is about three of us. The first is a twelve-year-old girl, one of the boat people crossing the Gulf of Siam. She was raped by a sea pirate, and after that she threw herself into the sea. The second person is the sea pirate, who was born in a remote village in Thailand. And the third person is me. I was not on the boat; I was tens of thousands of miles away, but because I was mindful, I knew what was going on in the Gulf. I was very angry, of course. But I could not take sides against the sea pirate. If I could have, it would have been easier, but I couldn't. I realized that if I had been born in his village and had lived a similar life—economic, educational, and so on—it is likely that I would now be that sea pirate. So it is not easy to take sides. Out of suffering, I wrote this poem. It is called "Please Call Me by My True Names," because I have many names, and when you call me by any of them, I have to say, "Yes."

> Do not say that I'll depart tomorrow
> because even today I still arrive.
>
> Look deeply: I arrive in every second
> to be a bud on a spring branch,

to be a tiny bird, whose wings are still fragile,
learning to sing in my new nest,
to be a caterpillar in the heart of a flower,
to be a jewel hiding itself in a stone.

I still arrive, in order to laugh and to cry,
in order to fear and to hope,
the rhythm of my heart is the birth and death
of all that are alive.

I am the mayfly
metamorphosing on the surface of the river.
and I am the bird which, when spring comes,
arrives in time to eat the mayfly.

I am the frog swimming happily
in the clear water of a pond,
and I am also the grass-snake who,
approaching in silence, feeds itself on the frog.

I am the child in Uganda, all skin and bones,
my legs as thin as bamboo sticks.
and I am the arms merchant,
selling deadly weapons to Uganda.

I am the 12-year-old girl, refugee on a small boat,
who throws herself into the ocean
after being raped by a sea pirate,
and I am the pirate,
my heart not yet capable of seeing and loving.

I am a member of the politburo,
with plenty of power in my hands.
and I am the man
who has to pay his "debt of blood" to my people,
dying slowly in a forced labor camp.

My joy is like Spring, so warm it makes flowers bloom.
My pain is like a river of tears,
so full it fills up the four oceans.

Please call me by my true names,
so I can hear all my cries and my laughs at once,
so I can see that my joy and pain are but one.

Please call me by my true names,
so I can wake up,
and so the door of my heart can be left open,
the door of compassion.

I still have the theme of this poem in my mind. "Where is our enemy?" I ask myself this all the time. Our earth, our green, beautiful earth, is in danger and all of us know it. We are not facing a pirate, but we are facing the destruction of the earth where our small boat has been. It will sink if we are not careful. We think that the enemy is the other, and that is why we can never see him. Everyone needs an enemy in order to survive. The Soviet Union needs an enemy. The United States needs an enemy. China needs an enemy. Vietnam needs an enemy. Everyone needs an enemy. Without an enemy we cannot survive. In order to rally people, governments need enemies. They want us to be afraid, to hate, so we will rally behind them. And if they do not have a real enemy, they will invent one in order to mobilize us. Yet there are people in the United States who have gone to the Soviet Union and discovered that the Russian people are very nice, and there are Soviet citizens who visit here, and when they return home, report that the American people are fine.

One friend in the peace movement told me, "Every time I see the President on television, I cannot bear it. I have to turn the TV off, or I become livid." I think I understand him. He believes that the situation of the world is in the hands of the government, and if only the President would change his policies, we would have peace. I told him that that is not entirely correct. The President is in each of us. We always deserve our government. In

Buddhism, we speak of interdependent origination. "This is, because that is. This is not, because that is not." Do our daily lives
have nothing to do with our government? I invite you to meditate
on this question. We seem to believe that our daily lives have
nothing to do with the situation of the world. But if we do not
change our daily lives, we cannot change the world.

In Japan, in the past, people took three hours to drink one
cup of tea. You might think this is a waste of time, because time
is money. But two people spending three hours drinking tea, being with each other, has to do with peace. The two men or two
women did not speak a lot. They exchanged only a word or two,
but they were really there, enjoying the time and the tea. They
really knew the tea and the presence of each other.

Nowadays, we allow only a few minutes for tea, or coffee. We
go into a cafe and order a cup of tea or coffee and listen to music
and other loud noises, thinking about the business we will trans-
act afterwards. In that situation, the tea does not exist. We are
violent to the tea. We do not recognize it as living reality, and
that it is related to why our situation is as it is. When we pick up
a Sunday newspaper, we should know that in order to print that
edition, which sometimes weighs 10 or 12 pounds, they had to
cut down a whole forest. We are destroying our earth without
knowing it.

Drinking a cup of tea, picking up a newspaper, using toilet
paper, all of these things have to do with peace. Nonviolence
can be called "awareness." We must be aware of what we are, of
who we are, and of what we are doing. When I became a novice
in a Buddhist monastery, I was taught to be aware of every act
during the day. Since then, I have been practicing mindfulness
and awareness. I used to think that practicing like that was only
important for beginners, that advanced people did other important things, but now I know that practicing awareness is for everyone, including the Abbot. The purpose of Buddhist meditation
is to see into your own nature and to become a Buddha. That can
be done only through awareness. If you are not aware of what is
going on in yourself and in the world, how can you see into your
own nature and become a Buddha?

The word "Buddha" comes from the root, *buddh*, which means "awake." A Buddha is one who is awake. Are we really awake in our daily lives? That is a question I invite you to think about. Are we awake when we drink tea? Are we awake when we pick up the newspaper? Are we awake when we eat ice cream?

Society makes it difficult to be awake. We know that 40,000 children in the Third World die every day of hunger, but we keep forgetting. The kind of society we live in makes us forgetful. That is why we need exercises for mindfulness. For example, a number of Buddhists I know refrain from eating a few times a week in order to remember the situation in the Third World.

One day I asked a Vietnamese refugee boy who was eating a bowl of rice, whether children in his country eat such high quality rice. He said, "No," because he knows the situation. He experienced hunger in Vietnam—he only ate dry potatoes and he longed for a bowl of rice. In France, he has been eating rice for a year, and sometimes he begins to forget. But when I ask him, he remembers. I cannot ask the same question of a French or American child, because they have not had that kind of experience. They cannot understand. I realize how difficult it is for the people who live in Western countries to know what the situation in the Third World really is. It seems to have nothing to do with the situation here. I told the Vietnamese boy that his rice comes from Thailand, and that most Thai children do not have this rice to eat. They eat rice of a poor quality, because the best rice is for export. Their government needs foreign currency, and they reserve the best rice for Westerners and not them.

In Vietnam we have a delicious banana called *chuối già*, but now children and adults in Vietnam do not have the right to eat these bananas because they are all for export to the Soviet Union. Do you know what we get in return? Guns, in order to kill ourselves and to kill our Cambodian brothers. Some of us practice this exercise of mindfulness: We sponsor a child in the Third World in order to get news from him or her, thus keeping in touch with the reality outside. We try many ways to be awake, but society keeps us forgetful. It is so difficult to practice awareness in this society.

A French economist named François Peroux, who is the head of the Institute of Applied Mathematics and Economics in Paris, said that if Western countries would reduce the consumption of meat and alcohol by 50%, that would be enough to change the fate of the Third World. How can we do it when we do not remember, to be aware? We are intelligent people, but we keep forgetting. Meditation is to remember.

There are means for us to nourish awareness, to enjoy silence, to enjoy the world. There was a 13-year-old boy from Holland who came to our Center and ate lunch with us in silence. It was the first time he had eaten a silent meal, and he was embarrassed. The silence was quite heavy. After the meal, I asked whether he felt uneasy, and he said, "Yes." So I explained that the reason we eat in silence is in order to enjoy the food and the presence of each other. If we talk a lot we cannot enjoy these things. I asked him if there was some time when he turned off the TV in order to better enjoy his dinner or the conversation with friends, and he said, "Yes." I invited him to join us for another meal, and he ate with us in silence, and enjoyed it very much.

We have lost our taste for silence. Every time we have a few minutes, we pick up a book to read, or make a telephone call, or turn on the TV. We do not know how to be ourselves without something else to accompany us. We have lost our taste for being alone. Society takes many things from us and destroys us with noises, smells, and so many distractions. The first thing for us to do is to return to ourselves in order to recover ourselves, to be our best. This is very important. We need to reorganize our daily lives so that we do not allow society to colonize us. We have to be independent. We have to be real persons and not just the victim of society and other people.

The boat people said that every time their small boats were caught in storms, they knew their lives were in danger. But if one person on the boat could keep calm and not panic, that was a great help for everyone. People would listen to him or her and keep serene, and there was a chance for the boat to survive the danger. Our Earth is like a small boat. Compared with the rest of the cosmos, it is a very small boat, and it is in danger of sinking. We need such a person to inspire us with calm confidence, to tell us what to do. Who is that person? The Mahayana Buddhist sutras tell us that you are that person. If you are yourself, if you are your best, then you are that person. Only with such a person— calm, lucid, aware—will our situation improve. I wish you good luck. Please be yourself. Please be that person.

There are so many peace organizations which do not have the spirit of peace themselves, and they even find it difficult working with other peace organizations. I think that if peaceworkers are really peaceful and happy, they will radiate peace themselves. To educate people for peace we have two alternatives: to use words, or to be peaceful ourselves and to speak with our lives and our bodies. I think the second way is more effective. One person is very important. I have seen such persons, and because of their way of living, they really influence others.

To take care of our children is also very important. Every time I look at a child, I think of the world we are going to leave for that child to live in. You know very well that if we are not peaceful, if we are not feeling well in our skin, we cannot raise our children well. To take good care of our children means to take good care of ourselves and to be aware of the situation we are in.

If we look deeply, we see that things are interrelated. If your daily life has not much to do with your government, then what does have to do with the government? That is a hard question. Has your daily life anything to do with the people who are dying in the Third World? This is the same question. During the Vietnam War, my countrymen fought not with weapons we had made ourselves—all the weapons came from somewhere else. In the U.S. the weapons industry still supplies the means for millions of people to kill each other. Do you think the existence of such an industry has to do with the situation of the world?

In our tradition, we are taught to look at things very deeply. For instance, if we look at a table, we can see a cloud, or a forest, or the sun in it, because without the cloud there would be no

water for the tree which became the table. We also see the logger and the wheat which made the bread for the logger to eat. In
the same way, if we look more deeply, we can see that our daily
life has very much to do with the situation of the world. The
President of the United States is in your daily life, not just in the
White House. Nonviolence is not a question of belief. It is a way
of life. It is awareness in order to have an accurate vision of
reality, and having an accurate vision of reality in order to be in
the most lucid state possible. From that basis, you can act.

It is very difficult to say that someone is nonviolent or violent.
We can only say that a person is more or less nonviolent at a
particular time. When I drink tea, I know that it is not entirely
nonviolent because in the cup there are many tiny living beings.
It is a question of direction. If you think that violence is sometimes needed, then I think you need more awareness and more
love. Then I am sure you will go in the other direction. Even a
General conducting a war can be more nonviolent or less violent. In planning strategies, he can avoid killing more people, so
there is a little bit of nonviolence in his violent act. You cannot
just separate people and say some are violent and some are not.
That is why people with love, compassion, and nonviolence
should be everywhere, even in the Pentagon, in order to encourage nonviolent attitudes within those we think are our enemies. That is why we have to love the President of the United
States. Otherwise we cannot influence him, we cannot encourage him to move in the direction of nonviolence.

I would like to suggest that in each home we have a small room
for breathing. We have rooms for sleeping, eating, and cooking,
why not have one room for breathing? Breathing is very important. I suggest that that room be decorated simply, and not be too
bright. You may want to have a small bell, with a beautiful sound,
a few cushions or chairs, and perhaps a vase of flowers to remind us of our true nature. Children can arrange flowers in
mindfulness, smiling. If your household has five members, you can
have five cushions or chairs, plus a few for guests. From time to

time, you might like to invite a guest to come and sit and breathe with you for a few minutes.

I know of families where children go into a room like that after breakfast, sit down and breathe ten times, in-out-one, in-out-two, in-out-three, and so on, before they go to school. This is a beautiful practice. Beginning the day with being a Buddha is a very nice way to start the day. If we are a Buddha in the morning and we try to nourish the Buddha throughout the day, we may be able to come home at the end of a day with a smile—the Buddha is still there. It is really beautiful to begin the day by being a Buddha. Each time we feel ourselves about to leave our Buddha, we can sit and breathe until we return to our true self. Doing these kinds of things can change our civilization.

THICH NHAT HANH

The Individual, Society, and Nature

When we speak of blossoms, leaves, and a tree, we distinguish between the blossoms, the leaves, and the tree which is the basis of their existence. But in reality, tree, flowers, and leaves are one, and belong to the same reality. The same is true when we speak of humanity and nature. We speak as though they do not belong to the same reality. In Chinese water and ink paintings, much space is always given to nature, and men and women are included as a part of nature. In the Buddhist tradition we are fond of using the expression *advaya* which means non-duality, the one and undivided, the unity of all things, the one reality. The Buddhist tradition, like many European traditions, encourages us to look at reality as a whole rather to cut it into separate entities.

When we look at a chair, for instance, our tendency is to separate it from the rest of the world, which might be called the non-chair world. And yet, our chair could not exist without its non-chair context. If we look carefully at our chair, we can see the whole world in it: the forest from which came its wood, the human race from which came the carpenter, and so on. If we remove all the non-chair elements from the chair, the chair will be unable to exist. Things in this world are interrelated. The Buddhist Genesis is summarized by this statement in the *Majjhimanikaya*: "This is because that is; this is not because that is not; this is born because that is born; this dies because that dies."

A human being is an animal, a part of nature. But we single ourselves out from the rest of nature. We classify other animals and living beings as nature, acting as if we ourselves are not part of it. Then we pose the question, "How should we deal with Nature?" We should deal with nature the way we should deal with ourselves! We should not harm ourselves; we should not harm nature. Harming nature is harming ourselves, and vice versa. If we knew how to deal with our self and with our fellow human beings, we would know how to deal with nature. Human beings and nature are inseparable. Therefore, by not caring properly for any one of these, we harm them all.

We can only be happy if we can make peace with ourselves. One should not presuppose that we, in our "natural" state, are in a state of peace already. The only thing we can do is to accept ourselves as we are, in order to begin to bring ourselves into harmony. A human being, according to Buddhism, includes a body, sensations, perceptions, mental formations, and consciousness. We must be aware of the functioning of all these in order to create harmony among them. Excess or abuse of any one disrupts peace. Physical illness and mental illness both result from a lack of understanding about what is going on in ourselves. If understanding the body is necessary to regularize and heal damage done by malfunctioning, understanding the mind is necessary for inner peace and mental health. This understanding helps us respect nature in ourselves and also helps us control and regularize it when necessary.

Causing harm to other human brings harm to ourselves. Accumulating wealth and owning excessive portions of the world's natural resources deprives fellow humans of the chance to live. Participating in oppressive and unjust social systems creates and deepens the gap between rich and poor, and aggravates the situation of social injustice. Yet while tolerating excess, injustice, and war, we usually are completely unaware that the human race suffers as a family. While the rest of the human family suffers and starves, enjoying false security and wealth can only be seen as a sign of insanity.

It has become clear that the fate of the individual is inextricably linked to the fate of the whole human race. People must let others live if they themselves want to live. ("This is because that is.") The only alternative to co-existence is co-non-existence. A civilization in which we must kill and exploit others in order to live is not a civilization of mental health. To create a civilization of mental health, all must be born truly equal: with the right to education, work, food, and shelter, to world citizenship, to freely circulate and settle on any part of the earth. Political and economic systems which deny anyone these rights harm the human family. Awareness of what is happening to the human family is necessary to repair the damage already done.

In order to make peace within the human family, we must work for harmonious co-existence. If we continue to shut ourselves off from the rest of the world, imprisoning ourselves in narrow concerns and immediate problems, we are not likely to make peace, or to survive. As in the case of the individual, preserving harmony in the human race is not easy. The human race is part of nature. We must gain an understanding of nature in the human race to bring it into harmony. Cruelty and disruption destroy the harmony of the human family, and destroy nature. Among the healing measures needed is legislation which does not do violence to ourselves or nature, but helps prevent us from being disruptive and cruel.

We have built a system which we cannot control. This system imposes itself upon us, and we have become its slaves and victims. Most of us, in order to have a house to live in, a car to drive, a refrigerator, television, and so on, must pledge our time and our lives in exchange. We are constantly under the threatening pressure of time. In former times, we could afford three hours for one cup of tea, enjoying the company of our friends in a serene and spiritual atmosphere. We could organize a party to celebrate the blossoming of one orchid in our garden. But we can no longer afford to do these things. We say that time is money. We have created a society in which the rich become richer and the poor become poorer, and in which we are so caught up in our own immediate problems that we cannot afford to be aware of what is going on with the rest of the human family.

The individual and all of humanity are both part of nature, and should be able to live in harmony with nature. Nature can be cruel and disruptive at moments, and therefore at times needs to be controlled. As in the case of individual humans and the human family, to control is not to dominate or to oppress but to harmonize and equilibrate. We must be deep friends with nature in order to control certain aspects of it. This requires a full understanding of nature. Typhoons, tornadoes, droughts, floods, volcanic eruptions, proliferations of harmful insects—all of these constitute danger and destruction to life. Although parts of nature, these things disrupt the harmony of nature. We should be able to prevent to a large degree the destruction such natural disasters cause. But we must do it in a way which preserves life and encourages harmony.

The excessive use of pesticides which kill all kinds of insects and upset the ecological balance is an example of our lack of wisdom in trying to control nature. Economic growth which devastates nature by polluting and exhausting non-renewable resources renders the earth impossible for beings to live on. Such economic growth may temporarily benefit some humans but in reality disrupts and destroys the whole of nature to which we belong.

The harmony and equilibrium in the individual, society, and nature are being destroyed. Individuals are sick, society is sick, nature is sick. The Way is to re-establish harmony and equilibrium. But how? Where should we begin the work of healing? In the individual, in society, or in the environment? It is easy to say that we must begin work in all three domains. People of different disciplines tend to stress their particular areas. For example, politicians consider an effective rearrangement of society necessary for the salvation of humans and nature, and therefore urge that everyone engage in the struggle to change political systems.

As a Buddhist monk, I, like psychiatrists, tend to look at the problem from the viewpoint of mental health. Buddhist meditation aims at creating harmony and equilibrium in the life of the individual. Buddhist meditation deals with both the body and the mind, using breathing as an effective tool to calm and harmonize the whole human being. As in any therapeutic practice, the patient is placed in an environment which favors the restoration of harmony. Often psychiatrists spend more time observing and then advising the mentally-ill patient. I know of some psychiatrists, however, who, like monks, observe themselves first of all, recognizing the necessity to free their own selves from the fears, anxieties, and despair that exist in each of us. Many psychiatrists tend to view themselves as if they had no mental problems, but the monk recognizes in himself the susceptibility to fears and anxieties, to the mental illness that is caused by the inhuman social and economic systems existing in the world today.

Buddhists believe that the reality of the individual, society, and nature's integral being will reveal itself to us as we recover, as we gradually cease to be possessed by anxiety, fear, and the dispersion of mind. Among the three—individual, society and nature—it is the individual who begins to effect change. But in order to effect change he or she must have personally recovered, must be whole. Since this requires an environment favorable to healing, he or she must seek the kind of lifestyle that is free from destructiveness. Efforts to change the environment and to change the individual are both necessary. But we know how difficult it is to change the environment if individuals are not in a state of equilibrium. From the mental health point of view, the efforts for us to recover our humanness should be given priority.

Restoring mental health does not mean simply adjusting individuals to the modern world of rapid economic growth. The world is ill, and adapting to an ill environment cannot bring real mental health. Many people who need psychotherapy are really victims of our modern life which separates human beings from the rest of the human family. One way to help such people may be to move them to societies where they will have the chance to cultivate the land, to grow their own food, to wash their clothes in the clear stream of a river, to live simply, sharing the same life as millions of peasants. Psychiatric treatment requires environmental change and psychiatrists must participate in efforts to change the environment, but that is only half the task. The other half is to help individuals be themselves, not by helping them adapt to an ill environment, but by providing them with the strength to change it. To tranquilize them is not the Way. The explosion of bombs, the burning of napalm, the violent death of our neighbors and relatives, the pressure of time, noise and pollution, the lonely crowds—these have all been created by the disruptive course of our economic growth. They are all sources of mental illness, and they must be ended. Anything we can do to end them is preventive medicine. And political activities are not the only means to end them.

While helping individually their own patients, psychiatrists must at the same time recognize their responsibility to the entire human family. The work of the psychiatrists must also prevent others from becoming ill. Psychiatrists are challenged to safeguard their own humanness. Like others, psychiatrists and monks need to turn their observation first of all to themselves and their own way of life. I believe that if they do just this, they will soon be seeking ways to disengage themselves from the present economic systems in order to engage themselves in efforts to re-establish harmony and balance in life. Monks and psychiatrists are human beings; we cannot escape mental illness if we do not apply our disciplines to ourselves. Caught in forgetfulness and acquiescence to the status quo, we will gradually become victims of fear, anxiety, and egotism of all kinds. I am confident that psychiatrists and monks, through mutual sharing, can help each other apply our disciplines to our lives in order to rediscover harmony.

A tree reveals itself to an artist when he or she can establish a certain relationship with the tree. If a human is not human enough, he may look at his fellow humans and not see them; he may look at a tree and not see it. Many of us cannot see things because we are not wholly ourselves. Wholly ourselves, we can see how one person by his or her way of living can demonstrate that life is possible, that a future for the world is possible. The question "Is a human future possible?" is meaningless without seeing the millions of our fellow humans who suffer, live, and die around us. Once we have really seen them, we can see ourselves, and we can see nature.

NELSON FOSTER

To Enter the Marketplace

THE POLITICS OF PRAJÑA

In the Nixon years, good years for paranoia, I used to joke that the FBI was infiltrating American Zen centers in an effort to squelch their subversive activities.[1] It was only a half-joke, really, because I see Zen practice as subversive in the deepest sense: it overturns distinctions which have been the very foundation of our attitudes, actions, and institutions. Most fundamentally, it shatters the premise of separateness that has guided our behavior since infancy. And with this, mysteriously, a revolution of the heart begins, turning the Zen student from self-concern toward concern for the welfare of others, from concern for the small self toward concern for the Self in which there are no "others."

Such a revolution is slow coming to fulfillment, for it entails a thorough realignment of character—changes in self-image, in habits of interaction, even in goals and desires. The great teachers warn, indeed, that the job is never finished.[2] A Japanese proverb points out that Shakyamuni Buddha himself is still only half-way there.

Yet slow as it is and different in its particulars for each of us, this course of change inexorably carries us all in the same direction—toward "entering the marketplace with helping hands."[3] In

47

terms of human development, compassion and generosity are the principal thrust of Zen practice. They are not its final stage, as is commonly thought, for it has no final stage. They are its final orientation, the true North of its compass, in keeping with the Mahayana ideal of the bodhisattva.

This being the case, it is remarkable that Zen lacks a clear tradition of social action. One searches in vain for a body of teaching equivalent to the "social gospel" of Christianity. In its history, we find isolated examples of people striking out on independent paths of social service and occasional instances of whole monasteries emptying to help a community recover from a disaster. In its scriptures, we find urgings toward poverty and lectures on the Bodhisattva Vows and the Precepts, which address life's largest ethical issues in ways that are congenial with social service. But there is no direct guidance about entering the marketplace with helping hands. Never has such guidance been more necessary than it is now, in our bewilderingly complex, highly integrated, technocratic society, and it seems that we need first to understand why it is missing and second to fill the void as well as we can.

Before examining these questions, I think it is helpful to recognize that we are talking about politics, which I define broadly as "the personal value systems and the social dynamics which together shape the decisions of any community, large or small, including the Buddhist community (sangha)." Few of us feel much relation with the tawdry circuses of ambition and greed that characterize politics in society at large, but it is important to acknowledge that daily life inevitably involves each of us in an unbroken and subtle net of political decisions and interactions.

Essentially, what I am suggesting is that Zen practice itself has a certain natural political bent: those of us who undertake Zen practice can expect to find our lives moved in the direction of social service. This is part of a larger phenomenon that I like to call "the politics of prajña"—the values orientation inherent to the experience of wisdom (prajña).

I do not mean to suggest that a moment of realization engraves a new set of values in one's heart. To repeat, practice and realization promote a process of personal change that is gradual and idiosyncratic, complicated by character and circumstance. Yet in fundamental ways, Zen meditation (*zazen*) works alike in all of us, and this is the source of the politics of prajña: When dualisms such as mine and yours, rare and common, precious and worthless, begin to lose their power, so must materialism. Anthropocentrism weakens in the same way, with the erosion of distinctions like animate and inanimate, advanced and primitive. Zazen, faithfully practiced, must inevitably undercut separation and chauvinism—racism, sexism, nationalism—and militate against exploitation or self-aggrandizement in any form.

If one accepts that Zen has such an implicit politics, it may seem all the more peculiar that it lacks a clear tradition of social service, but like other institutions, the Zen sect has been shaped as much by its environment as by its internal values. First, the generations of men and women who have come to Zen practice have inevitably brought with them the values of their societies, values more or less different from Zen's inherent values. Second, though it often took to the mountaintops in an effort to remove itself from the profane influences of city and state, the sect was subject to very powerful social forces. In short, as an institution, Zen has been able to express the politics of prajña only imperfectly, as embodied by people with cultural biases, in societies that placed certain constraints upon its development.

A brief review of the history of Zen may provide some understanding of how these environmental forces shaped the tradition we now inherit. To begin with, it is clear from the Pali texts, apocryphal or not, that early Buddhism was aware of itself as a force for social good. Shakyamuni appears in the Pali sutras as a peacemaker, provides guidelines for good rulership, criticizes India's caste system, emphasizes morality as the foundation of practice, and so forth. In southern Buddhism to this day, monks and nuns (and devout laypersons) play integral roles in villages and urban neighborhoods, not only as moral preceptors but also as leaders in community decisionmaking (i.e. politics).

As Buddhism moved into China, however, its social orientation changed quickly and thoroughly. Its commitment to service was maintained and, in a sense, heightened through articulation. The bodhisattva's commitment to postpone nirvana until all beings are enlightened is so lofty as to bear little apparent relation to the problems of everyday life, and while touting itself as the "Great Vehicle" Buddhism, the northern school never equalled the "Lesser Vehicle" in meeting the needs of public welfare.

This failure seems easy to comprehend in terms of the environmental pressures that Buddhism encountered in China. First, it was a guest religion in a society that viewed everything foreign as "barbarian." Under such circumstances, it is natural to minimize differences from the norm. Second, the established norm was Confucian, setting exacting expectations for the behavior of the religious, as for all others. Third, feudal and imperial authority were powerful, sufficiently powerful to ensure that institutions or individuals deviating from the norm were swiftly and effectively put in place. Gary Snyder has probably gone to the heart of the matter in observing that the Chinese world view (and later the Japanese) precluded a significant social role for Buddhism: the laws of heaven fixed the earthly order, and to stand against that order was folly.[4] War, famine, and the rise and fall of empire were understood much like weather—changing, but not subject to human intervention.

Whatever the precise dynamic, Chinese society effectively bottled up the social impulse in Buddhism and thereby set the direction of Zen, which was then defining itself for the first time as an institution. Confining the sangha's vitality within monastery walls created hothouse conditions, and one result was an extraordinary flowering of dialogues, poems, paintings, and commentaries which continue to delight and instruct us today. Another, less fortunate result was a diminution of the sangha's relationship with the society beyond its gates.[5]

In effect, the sangha "over-specialized" in wisdom and the arts. Besides being cloistered, it became esoteric and elite—doubly estranged from the surrounding community. Concerned with the preservation and elaboration of its genius, it devoted its resources to the enlightenment of its members and the growth and improvement of its monasteries. Building the institution became the dominant means of promoting the Dharma, and in pursuing this course, many abbots made the mistake of forming unholy alliances with the wealthy and the powerful. The pattern established in China was essentially duplicated in Korea and Japan. By the Kamakura Period, when the Buddhist elite had become part and parcel of Japanese power politics, and warrior-monks were commonplace in Zen temples, it took a monumental figure like Dogen to reject the favor of the court and to ban weapons from his monastery.

My purpose in reviewing this history is not to shower the old worthies with contempt, but rather to appreciate the dilemmas they faced and the choices they made. Certainly we cannot judge those choices by contemporary standards. The ancient teachers did not live in a world as ruined and miserable and precarious as ours. We cannot know how they would have responded had they felt the urgency of the atomic age.

But their actions have shaped modern Zen. To this day, Japanese Zen temples accept corporate contracts to train new employees in obedience, as in the past they welcomed samurai whose interest in Zen was confined to learning to kill and be killed with perfect equanimity.[6] Worse, the centuries of social constraint seem to have injected the poison of conformity into the very bloodstream of the Dharma. So it happens that a purported Zen master can applaud the publication of a koan answer-book containing this explanation of freedom: "To be free is to do what one is supposed to do without concern for what one could have done if..."[7] With this perversion of prajña, Zen's accommodation to its environment is complete; where such teaching is given, nothing will emerge from the temple but unquestioning, sterile obedience to social norms.

Fortunately, prajña itself does not die, and as long as zazen and realization are taught, an opportunity exists to renew the tradition we inherit. Indeed, as Zen moves west again, it enters a relatively open environment that may allow the sangha to live out its politics to a greater extent than ever before. With external constraints amounting to little more than the loose demands of neighborly courtesy and local ordinances, American Zen seems free to develop according to the lights of prajña.

Already American sanghas can be seen shattering some of the strictures that have bound Zen in Asia. The temple has become a locus of community work and play as well as a place for practice, rite, and instruction. In our distinctly non-Confucian circumstances, authoritarianism is drawing fire, with the general membership assuming an increasingly important role in decision-making at many centers. Sexism is waning, despite resistance. Vegetarianism is the norm. Concern for the natural world finds expression in simple living, recycling, gardening, and organic farming.

At several centers, direct service projects have also emerged. Social concern has prompted prison meditation projects, language instruction for immigrants, collections for disaster relief, efforts to rebuild inner-city community, work to end hunger and malnutrition, alternative health and child care, hospice support, refugee resettlement help, and more.

Some may argue that these developments have been shaped more by the American ethos than by free expression of the politics of prajña, but I think the argument ultimately fails. I find no evidence that the emerging culture of the American Zen sangha has been forced upon it as a protective adaptation to yet another foreign environment. Rather, the new forms seem to have taken root spontaneously, from within, as teachers and students found them helpful to express realization. After all, the values that have cropped up in the American sangha are hardly those that prevail in the population of the United States. The fact that our groups have moved in such similar directions, despite sectarian, geographic, and ethnic differences, suggests that our choices have been guided by values inherent to Zen.

This is satisfying: we can see that Zen's subversive force is affecting us individually and collectively, and it seems safe to assume that these effects are being felt beyond the circle of the sangha, in the society at large. As we bake and sell wholesome bread, meet Christians and Jews to explore common ground, or simply deepen our ability to greet strangers in the street, ripples of good influence spread outward from the temple. We are gently and perhaps unwittingly engaged in revolutionary activity—in that deep and slow reorientation of hearts which could turn civilization to a harmonious course.

Yet American Zen has largely ignored this subtle expression of its inner politics and has spurned more overt forms of social action. I think it would be healthy, for starters, to remind ourselves regularly that Zen practice does and should exert a quiet good influence on society. But I hope we can go farther, to agree that a place exists in American Zen for far more intentional efforts to embody the politics of prajña.

Really, we have no choice. Merely by living and thinking, we are involved in intentional political activity. Deciding not to vote expresses certain values, has political consequences, and must be recognized as a political act. Even as apparently non-political an act as consolidating sangha housing around the temple may have horrendous political consequences: in buying and occupying the desired dwellings, the sangha may contribute to "gentrification," pushing poor people into ever more squalid quarters. The real question is whether our behavior reflects prajña, not whether we engage in political behavior.

Much of this essay has been devoted to demonstrating that Zen's Asian heritage has created artificial impediments to the sangha's engagement in social service. If the American sangha will acknowledge that Zen's habit of conformity has stemmed from expedience, it will have come a long way toward agreeing that social service is integral to Zen practice. However, a number of other *common objections to social engagement* also need to be addressed:

1. *Overt social service would obstruct the sangha's paramount function of protecting and offering the Dharma.* —On the contrary, the foregoing glance at history seems to suggest that protecting and offering the Dharma require overt social involvement. The teaching itself is poisoned if it is not embodied in the world. The hungry need food dharma, the tortured need justice dharma, and the besieged

need peace dharma. If we can help and do not, then we have falsified the Dharma, and all our "protection of the teaching" is a vain, elitist exercise.

2. *Engagement in social issues runs counter to the Zen teaching of immediacy—or being completely present in this place at this moment.*
—The question is what this place-moment includes. Through our practice, we learn to forget ourselves in doing what we are doing, and the instant that our forgetfulness becomes complete, each of us realizes that there is only this in the whole universe. But such an experience of immediacy includes all beings in all dimensions of space and time, and to argue that our attention must be limited to the beings now within the radius of our senses is either corrupting the experience of immediacy or admitting that we have not had it. Practicing farther, seeing more clearly, it becomes apparent that the Central American rainforest is being destroyed right here and that the MARV missile is being built not only with my money but also with my hands.

3. *Religious practice is the only way to effect genuine change in ourselves and thus is the only way to create a better world.* —I think most of us who make zazen a way of life believe that religious practice is indispensable for profound and lasting harmony among the Earth's many beings. But it is an error to presume that less fundamental means of changing civilization have nothing to contribute. When proud and weary Rosa Parks kept her seat on an Alabama bus in 1955, she changed the world irrevocably for the better. Igniting the civil rights movement, she moved us all toward a just and peaceful future, and only a fool would wish that she had kept her seat in the church instead, never venturing into "politics." The gradual good influence of Zen is no match for the destructive forces afoot in society. It behooves us to work for harmony in any way that is itself harmonious.

4. *The processes of social action or political involvement are incompatible with Zen practice.* —Though run-of-the-mill politics is hardly conducive to practice and rarely consonant with the politics of pra-

jña, there is nothing about research, planning, debate, community organizing, public protest, and so forth that puts these activities inherently at odds with Zen. In the course of Zen study, one discovers that even a noisy argument is harmonious and complete and that forgetting oneself in the pros and cons of a difficult decision is true and complete Zen practice.

I don't mean to suggest that we should promote noisy arguments. On the contrary, we should search for forms of discussion and action that express our values. I recommend delving into consensus, nonviolence, tribal forms of organization, participatory democracy, and anarchism. These alternate means of group interaction offer ways to cooperate in our work and to avoid vanity, competition, exclusion, divisiveness, and other evils which infect politics-as-usual. They may also reveal ways to improve the decisionmaking structures at American Zen centers, which tend to conform to Asian assumptions about authority and power rather than to Zen's implicit politics.

5. *The forces that create injustice and violence are so large and our society is so complex that, however dedicated to service we may be, we cannot move effectively against them.* —We all know this feeling. Sometimes the politics of holding a job, eating, making a home, managing resources, paying taxes, maintaining relationships, and participating in the sangha seem quite enough to handle. Again, practice helps remove this barrier. Powerlessness dissolves in the experience of unity and emptiness that is zazen and realization. Powerlessness is, after all, a feeling, not a fact. The fact is that we do have power: A well-placed word may change someone's perspective. A trip to City Hall can unsnarl a bureaucratic tangle. Letters to the right person have opened many a prison door. And the thousands of individuals who joined the anti-war movement not only forced American troop withdrawal from Vietnam but also *prevented* use of nuclear weapons against Hanoi.

While I believe that nothing can long or legitimately stand between the American Zen student and vigorous social involvement, I have no blueprint for what that involvement should be. Prajña ingrains certain moral and behavioral tendencies, we can say, but the rest we must discover by intuition and induction. In the meantime, I find it easy to trust the process of growth that is already evident in our centers.

Just as sangha members' concern for children's welfare and for the needs of the sick have given rise to a sangha-supported school here or clinic there, so the organic development of Western Zen will inevitably bring forth sangha-supported ecology and disarmament groups. Of course, I hope this enlargement in the sangha's way of service will occur soon, and my words here have been intended to promote the process by removing mental obstacles that block the path. But no manifestos on the *dojo* doors, no stickers in the sutra books, no artificial politicization of the sangha are necessary or desirable.

Nor is there any need to set sangha-wide priorities for action. The turn toward service has taken many forms and will take many more, all helpful and none inherently better or worse than any other. There are likely to be critical practical considerations of needs and resources, and thought should be given to the depth of change a given project will promote. But there is no hierarchy of value by which the many possibilities for service should be judged.

It is important, too, that our paths of service not prove divisive for the sangha, as for the world at large. If our politics are divisive, they are not the politics of prajña. This requires us to distance explicitly political activity from the sangha—welcoming sangha participation but not expecting it and being clear with everyone that we act as individuals, not as representatives of our Zen centers. In this way, we reduce the risk of alienating others and ensure that people of all perspectives may feel at home in the meditation hall.

Finally, we need to appreciate the fact that intentional service is not for everyone, that it is fine if our friends—and even our teachers—refrain. To disrespect their choices is to violate our politics and, moreover, to give up on the slow, transforming effects of their zazen and our own helpful activity. We need to proceed, with or without the sangha's support, peaceful at heart, in the twin knowledge that good effects will unfold of themselves and that our intentional work in the marketplace will promote the change that the Earth so urgently needs.

LIKE SLEEPERS IN THE NIGHT

One aspect of the Zen temple I have always appreciated is that there one may say, along with other apparently sober people, "Though the many beings are numberless, I vow to save them." What a psychiatrist might regard as megalomaniac delusion or a child declare in superhero fantasy, we regularly recite as though it were perfectly ordinary.

In this connection, I think of the brilliant exchange set down in the 89th case of *The Blue Cliff Record*:

> Ungan asked Dogo, "How does the Bodhisattva Kanzeon use all those many hands and eyes?"
> Dogo answered, "It is like someone asleep adjusting the pillow in the middle of the night."

Kanzeon is Kuanyin, Avalokitesvara, the Bodhisattva of Compassion, and is commonly represented with four, seven, or eleven heads and up to a thousand arms. Further, Kanzeon is an archetype or, to put it directly, Kanzeon is each of us as the perfect embodiment of compassion, extending a thousand arms into the world of pain to save all beings.

So we may rephrase the question, "How do you yourself use all your myriad faculties?" and we can understand Dogo's answer to mean that we respond to the world's needs as a kind of reflex, a natural function of the silent mind, rather than as the end product of a complicated series of moral or logical decisions. We respond. In the long run, sophisticated moral and logical points will often be important to consider, but most intimately our response is an untutored impulse. In the authentic phrase of Yasutani Hakuun Roshi, "The compassion of the undifferentiated body of no-cause comes burning forth."[8]

Given our Zen practice, our common vow, and the natural working of compassion, it seems inevitable that in the past few years, as the chances and consequences of nuclear war grew ever more starkly apparent, Zen students would take action to protect the earth and its beings. And they did—through self-education and quiet organizing, vigils and street theater, leaflets and rallies, civil disobedience and door-to-door canvassing.

Yet only eight years ago it was not plain at all that this would happen. The Buddhist Peace Fellowship listed fifty or sixty Zen people among its members, some of whom were personally active in anti-nuclear work or other social concerns. But there was no consensus that such involvement was appropriate or necessary, and it was a rare sangha where a few people had gathered together to pursue their concerns in common. In an article written at that time, I felt compelled to argue that there is, in fact, a place in Western Zen for direct engagement in social service.

Now that Zen communities from New York to Honolulu have acted on their first vow in ways that are commonly called political, the time for such arguments is past: we have the tacit acknowledgement that practicing Zen and working for social change are not at odds. Yet I am troubled by indications that involvement in the anti-nuclear campaign is considered an exception to a general rule barring direct engagement in social concerns. At least one Zen teacher in the United States has explicitly endorsed activism on this issue only, and behavior at other centers—including rejection of feminist efforts in the sangha—suggests the exercise of similar restraint.

I suspect that this restraint arises from a devotion to the way Zen has traditionally worked in the world and a sense that the nuclear threat alone looms as a menace great enough to warrant deviation from this way. For centuries, Zen people have habitually abstained from overt social action, preferring to let subtle good influence radiate from the temple gate into the body of society, through a variety of means—a monk's model of selflessness, a teacher's influence on the ruler, the initiation of new cultural

forms like tea ceremony. Dr. Masao Abe aptly calls this
"dissolving the root of social evil" and contrasts it to cutting back
evil's branches through direct work for social or political
change.[9]

We who share a devotion to this deepest, gentlest way of
change may find it odious to admit that adhering strictly to it can
block the reflex of compassion and leave us powerless to meet
the problems of the present day. But admit it we must. Today it is
not only natural to respond to the cries of the world; it is also
necessary for our common survival.

The human capacity to bring suffering and destruction upon
ourselves and other beings has so broadened and accelerated
that change through religious experience cannot alone suffice to
save us. It is simply too slow. In the '70's, the world arms trade
quintupled, bringing on the hot, sophisticated warfare now consuming nation after nation throughout the Third World. By the
end of the '80's, as many as 15 countries could possess atomic
weapons. By the close of the century, even without a major military debacle, 60% of Earth's remaining forests may be gone—and
with them will go tens of thousands of plant and animal species,
fragile soil, and much of the planet's capacity to replenish its
oxygen supply.

Nuclear holocaust may be the most severe, universal threat the
world now faces, but we do not have the luxury of taking it on by
itself. It will do us little good to spare the Earth from nuclear destruction only to subject it to a final world war employing the lat-
est and most lethal conventional, chemical, biological, and laser
weapons. Nor will we have helped much if we permit the poisoning of the world with toxic wastes, wreak environmental
havoc by thinning the ozone layer, or let the Earth be destroyed
in the effort to secure scarce resources.

Huge structural forces are propelling us toward these disasters, despite millennia of religious faith and practice. Three of
the greatest Buddhist countries of all time—India, China, and
Japan—have each embraced nuclear power, nuclear arms, or
both; and none of them has devoted much attention to protecting
the biosphere, upon which everything depends. We delude our-

selves if we suppose that our zazen and its gentle good effects can alone have the corrective results that are now necessary for planetary survival.

Whether or not we agree that social action would be appropriate for Buddhists of other cultures or eras, it seems clear that it is appropriate in the West in these times. We must press for change in various ways, melding our religious and social powers in order to work purposefully and simultaneously at evil's root and branches. This fusion of spiritual insight and practical action has been achieved before and can be repeated, perfected, enlarged. While we may lack the strategic brilliance of Gandhi or the divine, cussed perseverance of Dorothy Day, surely we possess the intelligence to admire their examples and the capacity, by applying their teachings, to produce nonviolent change in our own environments. We also have the benefit of living guides similar in stature—Thich Nhat Hanh, Mother Teresa, Sulak Sivaraksa, A. T. Ariyaratne, Cesar Chavez—each of them showing in the quality of their words and deeds that engaging in world affairs may extend, not limit, religious devotion and practice.

Part of what we learn from their examples is that the burning energy of compassion must be governed by a lucid understanding of social problems and social change. Study, visitation, and analysis are tools they use often and well, but knowing suffering and discovering the means to end it seems usually to have demanded from them another kind of insight, more like the wisdom of religion than anything else. It is no accident that Gandhi sat a long time in his ashram before launching the historic Salt March. He was superbly educated and intimately acquainted with India's troubles, but these were not enough in themselves to provide the vision he needed.

This greater vision, it seems to me, rises from a meditative process akin to zazen. I am suggesting not that we employ zazen per se as a planning method but rather that the insight and discipline we take from it may serve us in finding our way to appropriate forms of action. If analysis is guided by a keen understanding of karma and a respect for silence and intuition, it will make a profound difference in the strategies we develop—a difference as great, I suspect, as the difference between a sentimental response to a baby's cry and the response of a parent who can distinguish the whimper of fatigue from a shriek of terror or a shout of hunger.

In complex socio-political matters, of course, achieving such vision is bound to be a relatively slow process. The question of how to rescue that screaming baby from an unfriendly dog is simple compared to the question of how to rescue several hundred thousand tribal people from extinction at the hands of an aggressive neighboring culture.

Yet it seems to me that meditators' attention to detail and ability to suspend conceptualization would give their action groups an edge over experts in analyzing and setting strategy on all but the most highly technical problems. In my work with the American Friends Service Committee, an international Quaker peace and development agency, I have learned that one or two relatively bright, open-minded, and patient observers produce more reliable analyses of current events than the media or the U.S. intelligence apparatus. Living in ordinary circumstances, watching events carefully, listening sensitively to people on all sides, and following the leadings of common sense—this is the sort of intelligence operation that promotes understanding and social service.

A good grasp of karma might provide an added asset. In examining the above phenomena, for example, without launching into a study of comparative data-gathering methods, we should be able to see the source of the CIA's problem: this leads to that. When you pay for information, you often receive what people think you want; when bias and fear lead you to trust certain kinds of sources and not others, developing a balanced view becomes nearly impossible; when your activity is secret, opportunities for normal interactions are reduced; and when great, weighty decisions depend on your reports, you may send fragments rather than a well-considered whole. This seems pretty simple, but evidently the CIA is not adept at karmic reasoning.

Whatever we may learn about analysis and planning, still there remains the question of where to bring one's efforts to bear, which apocalyptic force to challenge and at what level. Those who scrap the nuclear-only constraint will either replace it with something else or experience the burn-out and ineffectiveness that follows from adopting every stray cause that comes along.

Three alternative guidelines come to mind. "Nuclear war is bad for our practice," the tongue-in-cheek motto of a Buddhist Peace Fellowship group, suggests one possibility: to concentrate on countering those forces which seem to pose an ultimate threat to the survival of the Buddha Dharma; this can be seen as a logical and necessary extension of the ancient way of "dissolving the root" of social evil. A second possibility is for each group to focus on the sources of violence in its immediate vicinity—a local multinational corporation or a street gang perhaps, or a clear-cut lumber operation, a major polluter, a weapons merchant. A third option is to see if the group can agree on a form of violence that seems most fundamental—sexism or racism, perhaps—and let that agreement guide further choices.

Whatever group guideline is adopted, it is critical to respect the energies that each participant brings to the work. In many cases, planting a tree, riding the bus to work, or attending a single meeting will exhaust a friend's immediate energies for social change.

Those of us engaged in more time-consuming and perhaps finally more important forms of social service must be sure to appreciate others' gifts completely and genuinely, without any sense that they are somehow insufficient. Like any gift, these are small only if viewed with a mind of large and small. There is no right or wrong about where people stand on the continuum of social engagement; it is just like having brown, green, or blue eyes.

We also need to be generous in offering opportunities for people to get involved and in helping those who get overextended to reduce their responsibilities. Since individuals' capacity for such work varies widely, the most useful measure of appropriate involvement is internal: to do no more than one can do with clarity of mind and real devotion, and to help others do likewise.

Given the differences among us, differences from teacher to teacher and sangha to sangha, American Zen groups are unlikely to reach unanimity on the question of appropriate limits and means in fulfilling our vow to save all beings. This too is a matter of green eyes, blue eyes, and brown eyes. Not a bit of right or wrong.

Yet I would be dishonest if I smothered my growing confidence and hope that the American sangha will find its way broad enough to include active involvement in social change efforts of many kinds. It seems as inevitable as the recent wave of disarmament action: insight eats at our ignorance. We see that what harms one harms all, that what saves one saves all, that the joys and sorrows of today issue from our lives and return to them.

The knack for dispassion that we have acquired over the years fails us more and more. We realize that we have been living in a trance of abundance. We hurt with the many beings, and as their sufferings continue to worsen, we will reach out, as a matter of course, like sleepers in the night.

NOTES

[1]The two essays which comprise this article spring from concern about the reticence that new schools of American Zen have demonstrated in the realm of social action. Similar concern is felt by many Buddhists, in the old wave as well as in the new, in Europe as well as in the United States, in Vajrayana and Theravada traditions as well as in Zen, and I have been urged to revise the essays so that they speak to this wider audience. After several attempts, however, I find that I cannot make the leap; I feel comfortable addressing the issues only from my limited perspective as an American Zen student. Yet I would like to enlarge the dialogue about these problems, and I hope readers will translate whatever they find useful here into terms of reference appropriate to their experience.

[2]See, for example, Koun Yamada's commentary on Case 12 of the Mumonkan in his *Gateless Gate* (Los Angeles: Center Publications, 1979).

[3]Last of the "Ten Oxherding Pictures" by 12th century Chinese master Kuo-an Shih-yuan. See Philip Kapleau, *The Three Pillars of Zen* (Boston: Beacon Press, 1967), p. 311.

[4]"No Limit to the Size of the Garden," in *Blind Donkey* VIII, 4 (Honolulu, 1984).

[5]I do not mean to imply that Chinese masters all accepted this course of events. The very phrase "entering the marketplace with helping hands" originated in the 12th century (cf. n. 3, above). It is interesting to note, however, that the Oxherding Pictures center on a rustic, apparently a layperson rather than a monk. Perhaps even for Kuo-an's monks, the marketplace was out of bounds.

[6]Brian Daizen Victoria analyzes Japanese Zen's past and present socio-political role in his "Japanese Corporate Zen," Bulletin of Concerned Asian Scholars XII, 1 (Cambridge, 1980).

[7]Yoel Hoffman, trans., *The Sound of One Hand: 281 Zen Koans with Answers* (New York: Basic Books, 1975), p. 248. Commentary by the translator.

[8]Yasutani Hakuun, quoted in *Diamond Sangha* (Honolulu, July 1975), p. 39.

[9]"As Zen Comes to the West," *Blind Donkey* VIII, 1 (Honolulu, 1984), p. 19.

KEN JONES

Buddhism and Social Action:
An Exploration

It is the manifest suffering and folly in the world that invokes humane and compassionate social action in its many different forms. For Buddhists this situation raises fundamental and controversial questions. And here, also, Buddhism has implications of some significance for Christians, humanists, and other non-Buddhists.

By "social action" we mean the many different kinds of action intended to benefit humankind. These range from simple, individual acts of charity, teaching and training, organized kinds of service, "Right Livelihood" in and outside the helping professions, and through various kinds of community development as well as to political activity in working for a better society.

From the evidence of the Buddha's discourses, or suttas, in the *Digha Nikaya*, it is clear that early Buddhists were very much concerned with the creation of social conditions favorable to the individual cultivation of Buddhist values. An outstanding example of this, in later times, is the remarkable "welfare state" created by the Buddhist emperor, Asoka (B.C.E. 274-236). Walpola Rahula stated the situation—perhaps at its strongest—when he wrote that "Buddhism arose in India as a spiritual force against social injustices, against degrading superstitious rites, ceremonies and sacrifices; it denounced the tyranny of the caste system and advocated the equality of all men; it emancipated woman and gave her complete spiritual freedom."[1] The Buddhist scriptures do indicate the general direction of Buddhist social thinking, and to that extent they are suggestive for our own times. Nevertheless, it would be pedantic, and in some cases absurd, to apply directly to modern society social prescriptions detailed to meet the needs of a social order which flourished 23 centuries ago. The Buddhist householder of the *Sigalovada Sutta* experienced a different way of life from that of a computer consultant in Tokyo or an unemployed black youth in Liverpool. And the conditions which might favor their cultivation of the Middle Way must be secured by correspondingly different—and more complex—social, economic, and political strategies.

It is thus essential to attempt to distinguish between perennial Buddhism on the one hand and, on the other, the specific social prescriptions attributed to the historical Buddha which related the basic, perennial teaching to the specific conditions of his day. We believe that it is unscholarly to transfer the scriptural social teaching uncritically and without careful qualification to modern societies, or to proclaim that the Buddha was a democrat and an internationalist. The modern terms "democracy" and "internationalism" did not exist in the sense in which we understand them in the emergent feudal society in which the Buddha lived. Buddhism is ill-served in the long run by such special pleading. On the other hand, it is arguable that there are democratic and internationalist implications in the basic Buddhist teachings.

Buddhism offers to the individual human being a religious practice, a Way, leading to the transcendence of suffering. Buddhist social action arises from this practice and contributes to it. From suffering arises desire to end suffering. The secular humanistic activist sets himself the endless task of satisfying that desire, and perhaps hopes to end social suffering by constructing utopias. The Buddhist, on the other hand, is concerned ultimately with the transformation of desire. Hence he or she contemplates and experiences social action in a fundamentally different way from the secular activist. This way will not be readily comprehensible to the latter, and has helped give rise to the erroneous belief that Buddhism is indifferent to human suffering. One reason why the subject of this essay is so important to Buddhists is that they will have to start here if they are to begin to communicate effectively with non-Buddhist social activists. We should add, however, that although such communication may not be easy on the intellectual plane, at the level of feelings shared in compassionate social action experienced together, there may be little difficulty.

We have already suggested one source of the widespread belief that Buddhism is fatalistic and is indifferent to humanistic social action. This belief also appears to stem from a misunderstanding of the Buddhist law of karma. In fact, there is no justification for interpreting the Buddhist conception of karma as implying quietism and fatalism. The word karma (Pali: *kamma*) means volitional action in deeds, words, and thoughts which may be morally good or bad. To be sure, our actions are conditioned (more or less so), but they are not inescapably determined. Though human behavior and thought are all too often governed by deeply ingrained habits or powerful impulses, still there is always the potentiality of freedom—or, to be more exact, of a relative freedom of choice. To widen the range of that freedom is the primary task of Buddhist training and meditation.

The charge of fatalism is sometimes supported by reference to the alleged "social backwardness" of much of Asia. But this ignores the fact that such backwardness existed also in the West until comparatively recent times. Surely this backwardness and the alleged fatalistic acceptance of it stem from specific social and political conditions, which were too powerful for would-be reformers to contend with. Apart from these historic facts, it must be stressed here that the Buddha's message of compassion is certainly not indifferent to human suffering in any form; nor do Buddhists think that social misery cannot be remedied, at least partially. Though Buddhist realism does not believe in the Golden Age of a perfect society, nor in the permanence of social conditions, Buddhism strongly believes that social imperfections can be reduced, by the reduction of greed, hatred, and ignorance, and by compassionate action guided by wisdom.

From the many utterances of the Buddha, illustrative of our remarks, two may be quoted here:

> "He who has understanding and great wisdom does not think of harming himself or another, nor of harming both alike. He rather thinks of his own welfare, of that of others, of that of both, and of the welfare of the whole world. In that way one shows understanding and great wisdom."[2]

> "By protecting oneself (e.g., morally), one protects others; by protecting others, one protects oneself."[3]

Buddhism is essentially pragmatic. Buddhism is, in one sense, something that one does. It is a guide to the transformation of individual experience. In the traditional Buddhist teaching, the individual sets out with a karmic inheritance of established volitions, derived from his early life, from earlier lives, and certainly from his social environment, a part of his karmic inheritance. Nevertheless, the starting point is the individual experiencing of life, here and now.

Our train of argument began with the anxiety, the profound sense of unease felt by the individual in his or her naked experience of life in the world when not masked by busyness, objectives, diversions, and other confirmations and distractions. Buddhism teaches that all suffering, whether it be anxiety, or more explicitly karmic, brought-upon-ourselves suffering, or "external" suffering, accidental and inevitable through war, disease, old age, and so on—arise ultimately from the deluded belief in a substantial and enduring self. In that case, what need has the individual Buddhist for concern for other individuals, let alone for social action, since the prime task is to work on oneself in order to dissolve this delusion? Can one only then help others?

The answer to these questions is both yes and no. This does not mean half-way between yes and no. It means yes *and* no. It means that the answer to these fundamental questions of Buddhist social action cannot ultimately be logical or rational. For the Buddhist Middle Way is not the middle between two extremes, but the Middle Way which transcends the two extremes in a "higher" unity.

Different traditions of Buddhism offer different paths of spiritual practice. But all depend ultimately upon the individual becoming more deeply aware of the nature of his experience of the world, and especially of other people and hence of oneself and of the nature of this self. "To learn the way of the Buddha is to learn about oneself. To learn about oneself is to forget oneself. To forget oneself is to experience the world as pure object—to let fall one's own mind and body and the self-other mind and body."[4] Meditation both reveals and ultimately calms and clarifies the choppy seas and terrifying depths of the underlying emotional life. All the great traditions of spiritual practice, Buddhist and non-Buddhist, emphasize the importance of periods of withdrawal for meditation and reflection. Their relative importance is not our present concern. However, in all Buddhist traditions, the training emphasizes a vigilant mindfulness of mental feelings in the course of active daily life, as well as in periods of withdrawal. It also advocates the parallel development of habitual forms of ethical behavior (sila).

"We need not regard life as worth (either) boycotting or indulging in. Life situations are the food of awareness and mindfulness.... We wear out the shoe of samsara by walking on it through the practice of meditation."[5] The same message comes across forcefully in the Zen tradition: "For penetrating to the depths of one's true nature,...nothing can surpass the practice of Zen in the midst of activity....The power or wisdom obtained by practicing Zen in the world of action is like a rose that rises from the fire. The rose that rises from the midst of flames becomes all the more beautiful and fragrant the nearer the fire rages."[6]

It is open to us, if we wish, to extend our active daily life to include various possible forms of social action. This offers a strong, immediate kind of experience to which we can give our awareness practice. Less immediately, it serves to fertilize our meditation—"dung for the field of bodhi." Thirdly, it offers wider opportunities for the cultivation of *sila*—the habituation to a self-less ethic.

As we have noted, the significance of social action as mind-fulness training is, of course, incidental to that profound compas-sionate impulse which more—or less—leads us to seek the relief of the suffering of others. Our motives may be mixed, but to the extent that they are truly selfless they do manifest our potential for Awakening and our relatedness to all beings.

Through our practice, both in the world and in withdrawn meditation, the delusion of a struggling self becomes more and more transparent, and the conflicting opposites of good and bad, pain and pleasure, wealth and poverty, oppression and freedom are seen and understood in a Wisdom at once serene and vigi-lant. This Wisdom partakes of the sensitivity of the heart as well as the clarity of thought.

This Great Wisdom (*prajña*) exposes the delusion, the folly, sometimes heroic, sometimes base, of human struggle in the face of many kinds of suffering. This sense of folly fuses with the sense of shared humanity in the form of compassion (*karuna*). Compassion is the everyday face of Wisdom.

In individual spiritual practice though, some will incline to a Way of Compassion and others to a Way of Wisdom, but finally the two faculties need to be balanced, each complementing and ripening the other.

> He who clings to the Void
> And neglects Compassion
> Does not reach the highest stage.
> But he who practices only Compassion
> Does not gain release from the toils of existence.[7]

To summarize: Buddhist or non-Buddhist, it is our common humanity, our "Buddha nature," that moves us to compassion and to action for the relief of suffering. These stirrings arise from our underlying relatedness to all living things, from being brothers and sisters one to another. Buddhist spiritual practice, whether at work or in the meditation room, ripens alike the transcendental qualities of Compassion and Wisdom.

All social action is an act of giving (*dana*), but there is a direct act which we call charitable action, whether it be the UNESCO Relief Banker's Order or out all night with the destitutes' soup kitchen. Is there anything about Buddhism that should make it less concerned actively to maintain the caring society than is Christianity or humanism? "Whoever nurses the sick serves me," said the Buddha. In our more complex society does this not include the active advancement and defense of the principles of a national health service?

The old phrase "as cold as charity" recalls the numerous possibilities for self-deception in giving to others and in helping them. Here is opportunity to give out goodness in tangible form, both in our own eyes and those of the world. It may also be a temptation to impose our own ideas and standards from a position of patronage. David Brandon, who has written so well on the art of helping, reminds us that "respect is seeing the Buddha nature in the other person. It means perceiving the superficiality of positions of moral authority. The other person is as good as you. However untidy, unhygienic, poor, illiterate and blood-minded he may seem, he is worthy of your respect. He also has autonomy and purpose. He is another form of nature."[8]

There are many different ways in which individual Buddhists and their organizations can give help and receive suffering. However, "charity begins at home." If a Buddhist group or society fails to provide human warmth and active caring for all of its members in their occasional difficulties and troubles—though always with sensitivity and scrupulous respect for privacy—where then is its Buddhism? Where is the Sangha?

Political power may manifest and sustain social and economic structures which breed both material deprivation and spiritual degradation for millions of men and women. In many parts of the world, it oppresses a wide range of social groupings—national and racial minorities, women, the poor, homosexuals, liberal dissidents, and religious groups. Ultimately, political power finds its

most terrible expression in war, which reaches now to the possibility of global annihilation.

Contrariwise, political power may be used to fashion and sustain a society whose citizens are free to live in dignity and harmony and mutual respect, free of the degradation of poverty and
war. In such a society of good heart, *all* men and women find encouragement and support in making, if they will, the best use of
their human condition in the practice of wisdom and compassion. This is the land of good karma—not the end of human suffering, but the beginning of the end, the bodhisattva-land, the social embodiment of *sila*.

Buddhists are thus concerned with political action first, in the
direct relief of non-volitionally-caused suffering now and in the
future, and, secondly, with the creation of social karmic conditions favorable to the following of the Way that leads to the cessation also of volitionally-caused suffering, the creation of a society of a kind which tends to the ripening of wisdom and
compassion rather than the withering of them. In the third place,
political action, turbulent and ambiguous, is perhaps the most
potent of the "action meditations."

It is perhaps because of this potency that some Buddhist organizations ban political discussion of any kind, even at a scholarly
level, and especially any discussion of social action. There are
circumstances in which this may be a sound policy. Some
organizations and some individuals may not wish to handle such
an emotionally powerful experience which may prove to be divisive and stir up bad feeling which cannot be worked upon in
any positive way. This division would particularly tend to apply
to "party politics." On the other hand, such a discussion may give
an incomparable opportunity to work through conflict to a
shared wisdom. Different circumstances suggest different "skillful
means," but a dogmatic policy of total exclusion is likely to be ultimately unhelpful.

In this connection it is worth noting that any kind of social
activity which leads to the exercise of power or conflict may stir
up "the fires" in the same way as overtly political activity. Conflict
within a Buddhist organization is cut from the same cloth as

conflict in a political assembly and may be just as heady, but the Buddhist context could make such an activity a much more difficult and delusive meditation subject. The danger of dishonest collusion may be greater than that of honest collision (to borrow one of the Venerable Sangharakshita's aphorisms). The dogmatism and vehemence with which some Buddhists denounce and proscribe all political involvement is the same sad attitude as the dogmatism and vehemence of the politicians which they so rightly denounce.

Buddhism and politics meet at two levels—theory and practice. Buddhism has no explicit body of social and political theory comparable to its psychology of metaphysics. Nevertheless, a Buddhist political theory can be deduced primarily from basic Buddhism, from Dharma. Secondly, it can be deduced from the general orientation of scriptures which refer explicitly to a bygone time.

The writing of some Buddhists from Sri Lanka, Burma, and elsewhere offer interesting examples of attempts to relate Buddhism to nationalism and Marxism (not to be confused with communism). Earlier in the century, Anagarika Dharmapala stressed the social teaching of the Buddha and its value in liberating people from materialistic preoccupations. U Nu, the eminent Burmese Buddhist statesman, argued that socialism follows naturally from the ethical and social teachings of the Buddha, and another Burmese leader, U Ba Swe, held that Marxism is relative truth, Buddhism absolute truth. This theme has been explored more recently in Trevor Ling's book Buddha, Marx, and God [9] and Michal Edwardes' In the Blowing Out of a Flame.[10] Both are stimulating and controversial books. E. F. Schumacher's celebrated book, Small is Beautiful,[11] has introduced what he terms "Buddhist economics" and its urgent relevance to the modern world to many thousands of non-Buddhists. Of this we shall say more in a later section on the Buddhist "good society."

The First Precept of Buddhism is to abstain from taking life. But it must be made clear that the Buddhist "Precepts" are not commandments; they are "good resolutions," sincere aspirations voluntarily undertaken. They are signposts. They suggest to us how the truly Wise behave, beyond any sense of self and other.

Evil springs from delusion about our true nature as human beings, and it takes the characteristic forms of hatred, aggression, and driving acquisitiveness. These behaviors feed upon themselves and become strongly rooted, not only in individuals but in whole cultures. Total war is no more than their most spectacular and bloody expression. In Buddhism the cultivation of *sila* (habitual morality) by attempting to follow the Precepts is an aspiration towards breaking this karmic cycle. It is a first step towards dissolving the egocentricity of headstrong willfulness and cultivating heartfelt awareness of others. The Precepts invite us to loosen the grip, unclench the fist, and to aspire to open-handedness and open-heartedness. Whether, and to what extent, he keeps the Precepts is the responsibility of each individual. But he needs to be fully aware of what he is doing.

The karmic force of violent behavior will be affected by the circumstances in which it occurs. For example, a "diminished responsibility" may be argued in the case of conscripts forced to kill by an aggressive government. And there is surely a difference between wars of conquest and wars of defense. Ven. Walpola Rahula describes a war of national independence in Sri Lanka in the 2nd century B.C.E. conducted under the slogan "Not for kingdom but for Buddhism" and concludes that "to fight against a foreign invader for national independence became an established Buddhist tradition since freedom was essential to the spiritual as well as the material progress of the community."[12] We may deplore the historic destruction of the great Indian Buddhist heritage in the Middle Ages, undefended against the Mongol and Muslim invaders. It is important to note, however, that "according to Buddhism, there is nothing that can be called a 'just war'—which is only a false term coined and put into circulation to justify and excuse hatred, cruelty, violence and massacre."[13]

It is an unfortunate fact, well-documented by eminent scholars such as Edward Conze and Trevor Ling, that not only have avowedly Buddhist rulers undertaken violence and killing, but also monks of all traditions in Buddhism. Nonetheless, Bud⁺ dhism has no history of specifically religious wars, that is, wars fought to impose Buddhism upon reluctant believers.

Violence and killing are deeply corrupting in their effect upon all involved, and Buddhists will therefore try to avoid direct involvement in violent action or in earning their living in a way that, directly or indirectly, does violence. The Buddha specifically mentioned the trade in arms, in living beings, and in flesh.

The problem is whether, in today's "global village," we are not all in some degree responsible for war and violence to the extent that we refrain from any effort to diminish them. Can we refrain from killing a garden slug and yet refrain, for fear of "political involvement," from raising a voice against the nuclear arms race or the systematic torture of prisoners of conscience in many parts of the world? These are questions which are disturbing to some of those Buddhists who have a sensitive social and moral conscience. This is understandable. Yet, a well-informed Buddhist must not forget that moral responsibility, or karmic guilt, originate from a volitional and voluntary act affirming the harmful character of the act. If that affirmation is absent, neither the responsibility for the act, nor karmic guilt, rest with those who, through some form of pressure, participate in it. A slight guilt, however, might be involved if such participants yield too easily even to moderate pressure or do not make use of "escape routes" existing in these situations. But failure to protest publicly against injustice or wrongdoings does not necessarily constitute a participation in evil. Voices of protest should be raised when there is a chance that they are heard. But "voices in a wilderness" are futile, and silence, instead, is the better choice. It is futile, indeed, if a few well-meaning heads try to run against walls of rock stone that may yield only to bulldozers. It a sad fact that there are untold millions of our fellow-humans who do affirm violence and use it for a great variety of reasons (though not "reasonable reasons"!). They are unlikely to be moved by our protests or preachings, being entirely obsessed by diverse fanaticisms of power urges. This has to be accepted as an aspect of existential suffering. Yet there are still today some opportunities and nations where a Buddhist can and should work for the cause of peace and for reducing violence in human life. No efforts should be spared to convince people that violence does not solve problems or conflicts.

The great evil of violence is its separation unto death of us and them, of "my" righteousness and "your" evil. If you counter violence with violence, you will deepen that separation through thoughts of bitterness and revenge. The *Dhammapada* says: "Never by hatred is hatred appeased, but it is appeased by kindness. This is an eternal truth."[14] Buddhist nonviolent social action (*avihimsa, ahimsa*) seeks to communicate, persuade, and startle by moral example. "One should conquer anger through kindness, wickedness through goodness, selfishness through charity, and falsehood through truthfulness."[15]

The Buddha intervened personally on the field of battle, as in the dispute between the Sakyas and Koliyas over the waters of Rohini. Since that time, history has provided us with a host of examples of religiously-inspired, nonviolent social action, skillfully adapted to particular situations. These are worthy of deep contemplation.

Well known is the example of Mahatma Gandhi in the nonviolent struggle against religious intolerance and British rule in India, and also the Rev. Martin Luther King's leadership in the civil rights movement in the United States. A familiar situation for many people today is the mass demonstrations against authority, which may be conducted either peacefully or violently. As Robert Aitken has observed, "the point of disagreement, even the most fundamental disagreement, is still more superficial than the place of our common life." He recalls the case of a friend who organized an anti-nuclear demonstration at a naval base passing through a small town in which virtually every household had at least one person who gained his livelihood by working at the base. Consequently, when the friend visited every single house before the demonstration he hardly expected to win the people over to his cause. But he did convince them that he was a human being who was willing to listen to them and who had faith in them as human beings. "When we finally had our demonstration, with four thousand people walking through this tiny community, nobody resisted us, nobody threw rocks. They just stood and watched."[16]

And yet again, situations may arise in which folly is mutually conditioned, but where we must in some sense take sides in establishing the ultimate responsibility. If we do not speak out then, we bow only to the conditioned and accept the endlessness of suffering and the perpetuation of evil karma. The following lines were written a few days after Archbishop Oscar Romero, of the Central American republic of El Salvador, had been shot dead on the steps of his chapel. Romero had roundly condemned the armed leftist rebel factions for their daily killings and extortions. However, he also pointed out that these were the reactions of the common people being used as "a production force under the management of a privileged society....The gap between poverty and wealth is the main cause of our trouble....And sometimes it goes further: it is the hatred in the heart of the worker for his employer...If I did not denounce the killings and the way the army removes people and ransacks peasants' homes, I should be acquiescing in the violence."[17]

Finally there is a type of situation in which the truly massive folly of the conflict and of the contrasting evils may leave nothing to work with and there is space left only for personal sacrifice to bear witness to that folly. Such was the choice of the Buddhist monks who burnt themselves to death in the Vietnam war— surely one of the most savage and despairing conflicts of modern times, in which an heroic group of Buddhists had for some time struggled in vain to establish an alternative "third force."

The social order to which Buddhist social action is ultimately directed must be one that minimizes non-volitionally-caused suffering, whether in mind or body, and which also offers encouraging conditions for its citizens to see more clearly into their true nature and overcome their karmic inheritance. The Buddhist way is, with its compassion, its equanimity, its tolerance, its concern for self-reliance and individual responsibility, the most promising of all the models for the New Society which are on offer.

What is needed are political and economic relations and a technology which will: (a) Help people to overcome ego-centeredness, through cooperation with others, in place of either subordination and exploitation or the consequent sense of "righteous" struggle against these things.

(b) Offer to each a freedom which is conditional only upon the freedom and dignity of others, so that individuals may develop a self-reliant responsibility rather than being the conditioned animals of institutions and ideologies.[18]

The emphasis should be on the undogmatic acceptance of a diversity of tolerably compatible material and mental "ways," whether of individuals or of whole communities. There are no shortcuts to utopia, whether by "social engineering" or theocracy. The good society towards which we should aim should simply provide a means, an environment, in which different "ways," appropriate to different kinds of people, may be cultivated in mutual tolerance and understanding. A prescriptive commonwealth of saints is totally alien to Buddhism.

(c) The good society will concern itself primarily with the material and social conditions for personal growth, and only secondarily and dependently with material production. It is noteworthy that His Holiness the Dalai Lama, on his visit to the West in 1973, saw "nothing wrong with material progress provided man takes precedence over progress. In fact, it has been my firm belief that in order to solve human problems in all their dimensions, we must be able to combine and harmonize external material progress with inner mental development." The Dalai Lama contrasted the "many problems like poverty and disease, lack of education" in the East with the West, in which "the living standard is remarkably high, which is very important, very good." Yet he notes that despite these achievements there is "mental unrest," pollution, overcrowding, and other problems. "Our very life itself is a paradox, contradictory in many senses; whenever you have too much of one thing you have problems created by that. You always have extremes and therefore it is very important to try and find the middle way, to balance the two."[19]

(d) E. F. Schumacher has concisely expressed the essence of Buddhist economics as follows:

> While the materialist is mainly interested in goods, the Buddhist is mainly interested in liberation. But Buddhism is "The Middle Way" and therefore in no way antagonistic to physical well-being....The keynote of Buddhist economics is simplicity and nonviolence. From an economist's point of view, the marvel of the Buddhist way of life is the utter rationality of its pattern—amazingly small means leading to extraordinarily satisfying results.[20]

Schumacher then outlines a "Buddhist economics" in which production would be based on a middle range technology yielding on the one hand an adequate range of material goods (and no more), and on the other a harmony with the natural environment and its resources.[21]

The above principles suggest some kind of diverse and politically decentralized society, with cooperative management and ownership of productive wealth. It would be conceived on a human scale, whether in terms of size and complexity or organization or of environmental planning, and would use modern technology selectively rather than being used by it in the service of selfish interests. In Schumacher's words, "It is a question of finding the right path of development, the Middle Way, between materialist heedlessness and traditionalist immobility, in short, of finding Right Livelihood."

Clearly, all of the above must ultimately be conceived on a world scale. "Today we have become so interdependent and so closely connected with each other that without a sense of universal responsibility, irrespective of different ideologies and faiths, our very existence or survival would be difficult."[22] This statement underlines the importance of Buddhist internationalism and of social policy and social action conceived on a world scale.

The above is not offered as some kind of blueprint for utopia. Progress would be as conflict-ridden as the spiritual path of the ordinary Buddhist—and the world may never get there anyway. However, Buddhism is a very practical and pragmatic kind of idealism, and there is, as always, really no alternative but to try.

NOTES

[1]Walpola Rahula, Zen and the Taming of the Bull: Essays (London: Gordon Fraser, 1978).

[2]Anguttara Nikaya (Gradual Sayings), Fours, No. 186.

[3]Samyutta Nikaya (Kindred Sayings), 47; Satipatthana Samy, No. 19.

[4]Zen Master Dogen, Shobogenzo.

[5]Chögyam Trungpa, The Myth of Freedom and the Way of Meditation (Boston: Shambhala, 1976), p. 50.

[6]Philip B. Yampolsky, trans., Zen Master Hakuin (New York: Columbia University Press, 1971), p. 34.

[7]Saraha, Dohakosha (Treasury of Songs), in Edward Conze, ed., Buddhist Texts Through the Ages (New York: Harper & Row, 1964).

[8]David Brandon, Zen in the Art of Helping (London: Routledge & Kegan Paul, 1976), p. 59.

[9]2nd ed., Macmillan: London, 1979.

[10]Allen & Unwin, 1976.

[11]Blond & Briggs: London, 1973.

[12]Rahula, Op. Cit., p. 117.

[13]Rahula, What the Buddha Taught (New York: Grove Press, 1974), p. 84.

[14]Dhammapada I, 5.

[15]*Dhammapada*, XVII.

[16]*Ten Directions*, Los Angeles Zen Center, 1, 3, Sept. 1980, p. 6.

[17]*The Observer*, London, 30 March 1980.

[18]See *Buddhism and Democracy*, Bodhi Leaves, No. B., 17.

[19]Dalai Lama, *Universal Responsibility and the Good Heart* (Dharamsala, India: Library of Tibetan Works, 1976), pp. 10, 14, 29.

[20]Schumacher, *Op. Cit.*, p. 52.

[21]See also Dr. Padmasiri de Silva's pamphlet *The Search for a Buddhist Economics*, in the series, Bodhi Leaves, No. B. 69.

[22]Dalai Lama, *Op. Cit.*, pp. 5, 28.

GARY SNYDER

Buddhism and the Possibilities of a Planetary Culture

Buddhism holds that the universe and all creatures in it are intrinsically in a state of complete wisdom, love, and compassion, acting in natural response and mutual interdependence. The personal realization of this from-the-beginning state cannot be had for and by one-"self,"—because it is not fully realized unless one has given the self up and away.

In the Buddhist view, that which obstructs the effortless manifestation of this is Ignorance, which projects into fear and needless craving. Historically, Buddhist philosophers have failed to analyze out the degree to which ignorance and suffering are caused or encouraged by social factors, considering fear-and-desire to be given facts of the human condition. Consequently the major concern of Buddhist philosophy is epistemology and "psychology" with no attention paid to historical or sociological problems. Although Mahayana Buddhism has a grand vision of universal salvation, the actual achievement of Buddhism has been the development of practical systems of meditation toward the end of liberating a few dedicated individuals from psychological hangups and cultural conditionings. Institutional

Buddhism has been conspicuously ready to accept or ignore the inequalities and tyrannies of whatever political system it found itself under. This can be death to Buddhism, because it is death to any meaningful function of compassion. Wisdom without compassion feels no pain.

No one today can afford to be innocent, or to indulge themselves in ignorance of the nature of contemporary governments, politics, and social orders. The national polities of the modern world are "states" which maintain their existence by deliberately fostered craving and fear: monstrous protection rackets. The "free world" has become economically dependent on a fantastic system of stimulation of greed which cannot be fulfilled, sexual desire which cannot be satiated, and hatred which has no outlet except against oneself, the persons one is supposed to love, or the revolutionary aspirations of pitiful, poverty-stricken marginal societies. The conditions of the Cold War have turned most modern societies—both Soviet and capitalist—into vicious distorters of true human potential. They try to create populations of *preta*—hungry ghosts, with giant appetites and throats no bigger than needles. The soil, the forests, and all animal life are being consumed by these cancerous collectivities; the air and water of the planet is being fouled by them.

There is nothing in human nature or the requirements of human social organization which intrinsically requires that a society be contradictory, repressive, and productive of violent and frustrated personalities. Findings in anthropology and psychology make this more and more evident. One can prove it for oneself by taking a good look at Original Nature through meditation. Once a person has this much faith and insight, one will be led to a deep concern with the need for radical social change through a variety of nonviolent means.

The joyous and voluntary poverty of Buddhism becomes a positive force. The traditional harmlessness and avoidance of taking life in any form has nation-shaking implications. The practice of meditation, for which one needs only "the ground beneath one's feet," wipes out mountains of junk being pumped into the mind by the mass media and supermarket universities. The belief in a serene and generous fulfillment of natural loving desires destroys ideologies which blind, maim, and repress—and points the way to a kind of community which would amaze "moralists" and transform armies of men who are fighters because they cannot be lovers.

Avatamsaka (*Kegon* or *Hua-yen*) Buddhist philosophy sees the world as a vast, interrelated network in which all objects and creatures are necessary and illuminated. From one standpoint, governments, wars, or all that we consider "evil" are uncompromisingly contained in this totalistic realm. The hawk, the swoop, and the hare are one. From the 'human" standpoint we cannot live in those terms unless all beings see with the same enlightened eye. The Bodhisattva lives by the sufferer's standard, and he or she must be effective in aiding those who suffer.

The mercy of the West has been social revolution; the mercy of the East has been individual insight into the basic self/void. We need both. They are both contained in the traditional three aspects of the Dharma path: wisdom (*prajña*), meditation (*dhyana*), and morality (*sila*). Wisdom is intuitive knowledge of the mind of love and clarity that lies beneath one's ego-driven anxieties and aggressions. Meditation is going into the mind to see this for yourself—over and over again, until it becomes the mind you live in. Morality is bringing it back out in the way you live, through personal example and responsible action, ultimately toward the true community (*sangha*) of "all beings." This last aspect means, for me, supporting any cultural and economic revolution that moves clearly toward a truly free world. It means using such means as civil disobedience, outspoken criticism, protest, pacifism, voluntary poverty, and even gentle violence if it comes to a matter of restraining some impetuous crazy. It means affirming the widest possible spectrum of non-harmful individual behavior—defending the right of individuals to smoke hemp, eat peyote, be polygamous, polyandrous, or homosexual. Worlds of behavior and custom long banned by the Judaeo-Capitalist-Christian-Marxist West. It means respecting intelligence and learning, but not as greed or means to personal power. Working on one's own responsibility, but willing to work with a group. "Forming the new society within the shell of the old"—the I.W.W. slogan of 70 years ago.

The traditional, vernacular, primitive, and village cultures may appear to be doomed. We must defend and support them as we would the diversity of ecosystems; they are all manifestations of Mind. Some of the elder societies accomplished a condition of Sangha, with not a little of Buddha and Dharma as well. We touch base with the deep mind of peoples of all times and places in our meditation practice, and this is an amazing revolutionary aspect of the Buddhadharma. By a "planetary culture" I mean the kind of societies that would follow on a new understanding of that relatively recent institution, the National State, an understanding that might enable us to leave it behind. The State is greed made legal, with a monopoly on violence; a natural society is familial and cautionary. A natural society is one which "Follows the Way," imperfectly but authentically.

Such an understanding will close the circle and link us in many ways with the most creative aspects of our archaic past. If we are lucky, we may eventually arrive at a world of relatively mutually tolerant small societies attuned to their local natural region and united overall by a profound respect and love for the mind and nature of the universe.

I can imagine further virtues in a world sponsoring societies with matrilineal descent, free-form marriage, "natural credit" economics, far less population, and much more wilderness.

ROBERT AITKEN

Gandhi, Dogen, and Deep Ecology

A friend once inquired if Gandhi's aim in settling in the village and serving the villagers as best he could was purely humanitarian. Gandhi replied, "I am here to serve no one else but myself, to find my own self-realization through the service of these village folks."[1]

This remarkable conversation reveals Gandhi's stature as a world teacher. It is a true *mondo*, with the enlightened one responding to the fixed attitude of the questioner, turning the question around and using it as a vehicle for showing the truth that the question in its original form actually obscured.

The question was asked, not without malice, from the conventional suspicion of generosity: Isn't everything you do for others really a way of aggrandizing yourself? Is there really such a thing as pure generosity? Is it possible to live just for others? Aren't you serving your own psychological needs by living with poor people like this?

Gandhi replied from a point of view that is not conventional. He omits the word "humanitarian" entirely from his reply, and indeed I wonder if it is found anywhere in his writings or speeches. For the questioner, humanitarianism seems unrealistic, and in effect Gandhi acknowledges this, agreeing in order to make a deeper point.

Like a judo expert, Gandhi uses the energy and thrust of the other. Challenged to deny that he is just serving himself, he does not deny it at all, but takes the challenge a step further and states clearly that the villagers are serving him.

This is not self-aggrandizement, but the way of self-realization, as Gandhi says. Ego-concerns vanish, and the true nature of the one who observes and takes action becomes clear. It is none other than all beings and all things. Thomas Merton observes that Gandhi's practice was the awakening of India and of the world within himself[2]—or, I would say, as himself. Merton obviously felt this was an existential awakening, but whether it was existential or merely political, the truth remains: the other is no other than myself.

The conventional view that serving others is a means for self-aggrandizement is the view that accepts exploitation of people and the environment, wars between nations, and conflicts within the family. As Yasutani Hakuun Roshi used to say, the fundamental delusion of humanity is to suppose that I am here, and you are out there.

Gandhi's view is traditionally Eastern and is found with differing emphases in Hinduism, Taoism, and in Theravada and Mahayana Buddhism. For Dogen Zenji and for Zen Buddhists generally, the way is openness to all beings, all things. Each being confirms my self-nature, but if I seek to control the other, I fall into delusion:

> That the self advances and confirms the myriad things is called delusion. That the myriad things advance and confirm the self is enlightenment.[3]

The self imposing upon the other is not only something called delusion, it is the ruination of our planet and all of its creatures. But enlightenment is not just a matter of learning from another human being. When the self is forgotten, it is recreated again and again, ever more richly, by the myriad things and beings of the universe:

> The wild deer, wand'ring here & there,
> Keeps the Human Soul from Care.[4]

This is not just a matter of sensing the oneness of the universe. Stars of a tropical sky spread across the ceiling of my mind, and the cool wind unlocks my car.

Such experiences are not philosophy, and are not confined to the traditional East, but in the past two hundred years, east or west, we must look to the periphery of our culture, rather than to the mainstream, to find anything similar. The mainstream follows a utilitarian interpretation of God's instructions to Noah:

> And the fear of you and the dread of you shall be upon every beast of the earth, and upon every fowl of the air, and upon all that moveth on the earth, and upon all the fishes of the sea; into your hand they are delivered.[5]

It is only a very few, relatively isolated geniuses in the west, such as Wordsworth and Thoreau, who taught confirmation of the human self by nature, and the crime of confirming nature by the self. For example, here Wordsworth echoes Dogen:

> Think you, 'mid all this mighty sum
> Of things forever speaking,
> That nothing of itself will come,
> But we must still be seeking?[6]

Openness to the myriad things follows what George Sessions, in his discussion of deep ecology, calls conversion:

> The forester ecologist Aldo Leopold underwent a dramatic conversion from the "stewardship" shallow ecology resource-management mentality of man-over-nature to announce that humans should see themselves realistically as "plain members" of the biotic community. After the conversion, Leopold saw steadily and with "shining clarity" as he broke through the anthropocentric illusions of his time and began "thinking like a mountain."[7]

Man-over-nature is the self advancing and confirming the myriad things, an anthropocentric delusion. It is the same mindset as Americans over Vietnamese, or men over women, or managers over workers, or whites over blacks.

The Deep Ecology movement has grown out of the despair of ecologists over the conventional resource-management mentality which is rapidly depleting our minerals, razing our forests, and poisoning our rivers and lakes. It is precisely the same as the welfare society mentality that manages human resources for the short-term benefit of the managers themselves.

Readers of the conventional media have more awareness of the dangers of war and nuclear poison than they have of the biological holocaust involved in clearing jungles, strip mining mountains, disrupting the balance of life in the oceans, and draining coastal swamps. One must read the journals and bulletins of ecological societies to gain a perspective of the accelerating global disaster that our luxurious way of life is bringing down upon us all.

But even with knowledge, I wonder if it would be possible to reverse the machine of death and destruction. We in the peace movement have sought to levitate the Pentagon, falling into the same delusion that Dogen Zenji warns us about. When we stopped the B-1 Bomber, we got the Cruise Missile. When we stopped the Omnibus Crime Bill, we got another Omnibus Crime Bill. When we stopped LBJ, we got Richard Nixon.

The point is that, with all our good intentions, we are still seeking to advance and control the myriad things. The alternative is not just to respond passively or to run away. Once one thinks like a mountain, the whole world is converted. All things confirm me. Then I sit on dojo cushions which do not move. There is no controller and no one to control. Erik H. Erikson suggests that Gandhi held fast to his values to the exclusion of human needs in his family and even in his nation.[8] Probably so. We need not venerate him blindly. With all his flaws, he was surely a forerunner of a New Reformation that seeks to encourage self-sufficiency and also personal responsibility for all beings and all things.

In the Buddhist world we have in the past generation seen the development of Sarvodaya Shramadana in Sri Lanka, the Coordinating Group for Religion in Society in Thailand, the School of Youth for Social Service in South Vietnam, and Ittoen in Japan. These movements developed in the modern *zeitgeist* of social consciousness and have found guidance in the Buddhist doctrine of non-ego and in the Buddhist precepts, just as Gandhi could find guidance for the Indian independence movement in the ancient Hindu doctrine of self-reliance.

In the Christian world, we have seen the rise of similar movements, notably the Catholic Worker, an anarchist network of communal houses in dozens of American cities, set up by families of laymen and laywomen to feed the poor, clothe them, and shelter them, just as Jesus taught: "Inasmuch as you have done it to one of the least of these, my brothers and sisters, you have done it to me."9

These movements grew from their roots with the realization that confirmation by the myriad things is not just an esoteric experience confined within monastery walls. Swaraj, or independence, was for Gandhi the self-reliance of individuals who practiced the way of realization by complete openness to the British, the ultimate "other" for colonial India. It is also, as Gandhi indicated to the one who questioned his humanitarianism, the practice of being with the poor, the handicapped, the oppressed, thinking as they do, drawing water and digging the earth as they do. It is the practice of realization through their service—and through the service of all others, including police and politicians.

The practice of "being with them" converts the third person, *they, it, she, he,* into the first person *I,* and *we.* For Dogen Zenji, the others who are "none other than myself" include mountains, rivers, and the great earth. When one thinks like a mountain, one thinks also like the black bear, and this is a step beyond Gandhi's usual concerns to deep ecology, which requires openness to the black bear, becoming truly intimate with him.

This is compassion, suffering with others. "Dwell nowhere, and bring forth that mind." "Nowhere" is the zero of purest experience, known inwardly as fundamental peace and rest. To "come forth" is to stand firmly and contain the myriad things. For the peace or ecology worker, the message of the *Diamond Sutra* would be: "From that place of fundamental peace, come forth as a man or woman of peace, presenting peace in the inmost community of those who would destroy it."

NOTES

Thanks to George Sessions, whose paper, "Spinoza, Perennial Philosophy, and Deep Ecology," was a direct inspiration for this essay. (Mimeo., Sierra College, Rocklin, California, 1979). I am told that Arne Naess, the Norwegian eco-philosopher who coined the term, "deep ecology," is now using the expression, "New Philosophy of Nature," as something less divisive and invidious.

[1] Jag Parvesh Chander, *Teachings of Mahatma Gandhi* (Lahore: The India Book Works, 1945), p. 375, (Tähtinen, *Non-violence as an Ethical Principle*, p. 83).

[2] Thomas Merton, *Gandhi on Non-violence* (New York: New Directions, 1965), p. 5.

[3] See Maezumi, *The Way of Everyday Life* (Los Angeles: Center Publications, 1978).

[4] Blake, "Auguries of Innocence," *Poetry and Prose of William Blake*, p. 118.

[5] Genesis 9:2.

[6] William Wordsworth, "Expostulation and Reply," *Lyrical Ballads*, ed W. J. B. Owens (New York: Oxford University Press, 1967), p. 104.

[7] Sessions, "Spinoza, Perennial Philosophy, and Deep Ecology," p. 15. Space is too limited for a complete discussion of deep ecology, which naturally must include provision for agriculture and other kinds of environmental management. It is the mind-set that would exploit the future and exterminate species that the ecophilosophers wish to see turned around.

[8]Erik H. Erikson, *Gandhi's Truth: On the Origins of Militant Non-violence* (New York: Norton, 1969), especially p. 251.

[9]Matthew 25:40.

CHAGDUD TULKU

The Power of Peace

It is my wish that the spiritual power of peace will touch the mind of every person on this earth, radiating out from a deep peace within our own minds, across political and religious barriers, across the barriers of ego and conceptual righteousness. Our first work as peacemakers is to clear our minds of mental conflicts caused by ignorance, anger, grasping, jealousy, and pride. Spiritual teachers can guide us in the purification of these poisons, and through this purification of our own minds, we can learn the very essence of peacemaking.

The inner peace we seek should be so absolutely pure, so stable, that it cannot be moved to anger by those who live and profit by war, or to self-grasping and fear by confrontation with contempt, hatred, and death. Incredible patience is necessary to accomplish any aspect of world peace, and the source of such patience is the space of inner peace from which you recognize with great clarity that war and suffering are the outer reflections of the minds' inner poisons.

If you truly understand that the essential difference in peacemakers and warmakers is that peacemakers have discipline and control over egotistical anger, grasping, jealousy, and pride, while warmakers, in their ignorance, manifest the results of these poisons in the world—if you truly understand this you will never allow yourself to be defeated from within or without.

Tibetan Buddhists use the peacock as the symbol for the Bodhisattva, the Awakened Warrior who works for the Enlightenment of all sentient beings. The peacock is said to eat poisonous plants and transmute them into the gorgeous colors of its feathers. It does not poison itself, just as we who wish for world peace must not poison ourselves.

As you meet the powerful, worldly men who sit at the top of the war machines, regard them with strict equanimity. Convince them as effectively as you know how, but be constantly aware of your own state of mind. If you begin to experience anger, retreat. If you can go on without anger, perhaps you will penetrate the terrible delusion that causes war and all its hellish sufferings. From the clear space of your own inner peace, your compassion must expand to include all who are involved in war—the soldiers caught in the cruel karma of killing, and who sacrifice their precious human rebirth; the generals and politicians who intend to benefit but cause disruption and death instead; the civilians who are wounded, killed, and turned into refugees. True compassion is utterly neutral and is moved by suffering of every sort, not tied to right and wrong, attachment and aversion.

The work of peace is a spiritual path in itself, a means to develop perfect qualities of mind and to test these qualities against urgent necessity, extreme suffering and death. Do not be afraid to give your time, energy, and wealth.

Exemplars of Engaged Buddhism

RAFE MARTIN

Thoughts on the Jatakas

The Jataka tales (*jataka* simply means "birthlet"), or tales of the Buddha's earlier births, are the record, through countless lifetimes, of both the historical Buddha's and any ripening Bodhisattva's compassionate and often heroic self-giving. Two major collections of such tales have come down to us. Five hundred fifty tales are retained in the classic Pali *Jataka* and another 35, with some overlap from the *Jataka*, in the Sanskrit *Jatakamala* (or "Garland of Jatakas") of Aryashura. These written records are just a small portion of a much larger oral tradition of *avadana* ("noble deed" or "noble giving") literature which has largely vanished. The Jatakas themselves, in written, oral, and dramatic forms, have persisted through the centuries and have been immensely popular in all the traditional Buddhist countries. Indeed, many of the greatest Buddhist monuments of Asia are carved and painted with hundreds of scenes from the Jatakas.

The Pali *Jataka* contains many kinds and levels of tales from monkish moralizings and simple animal fables, to moving and compassionate animal-birth stories and fragments of larger heroic epics. Each is accompanied by a verse, which is canonical. Tradition asserts that all these verses and tales were told by the Buddha himself as a way of explaining a particular life situation of concern to his monks and lay followers at that moment.

Taking the current incident (traditionally titled "The Story of the Present"), he told a tale of one of his own earlier births ("The Story of the Past") which revealed the karmic origins of the situation at hand. The *Jatakamala* is a more literary, devotional, and centrally Mahayana work. Its core is the bodhisattva ideal. In it, tales of compassion and self-sacrifice are given thematic pre-eminence.

In both collections, however, the Buddha is shown not as withdrawing from the world, but as acting with compassion and wisdom for the benefit of all living beings. These untold lifetimes of effort, caring, and self-sacrifice, then, underlay his six years of ardent formal meditation practice when as the ex-Prince Siddhartha, he at last attained his long-sought goal of Buddhahood. Just prior to his final Enlightenment, legend records that Mara, the tempter, appeared before the future Buddha and asked him if he was truly worthy of attaining so high a goal. In response, the he touched the earth lightly with his right hand asking the humble earth to witness for him. The earth replied, "He is worthy! There is not a single spot on this globe where, through countless lifetimes, he has not offered his own life for the welfare of others!" All those past lives to which the earth bore witness are the lives recorded in the Jatakas. They are the hidden foundation upon which the Buddha's great, historical attainment necessarily stands.

In the Jatakas we discover the essence of the Buddhist attitude brought to life—the attitude of universal compassion which Lama Govinda describes as "the spontaneous urge to help others flowing from the knowledge of inner oneness." Elsewhere he also says that:

> ... the way of the Buddha was not one of running away from the world, but of overcoming it through growing knowledge (*prajña*), through active love (*maitri*) towards one's fellow beings, through inner participation in the joys and sufferings of others (*karuna muditha*), and equanimity with regard to one's own weal and woe. This way was vividly illustrated by the innumerable forms of

existence of the Buddha (up to his last as Gautama Shakyamuni), as told in the Jatakas.

In the Jatakas, we learn that, long ago, as a Deer King, the Buddha risked his own life to free all creatures from danger; as a monkey he saved an ungrateful hunter; as a lion he saved all the frightened beasts from their own fears; as a parrot he flew self-lessly through flames to save all those trapped in a burning forest; as an elephant he offered his life so that starving men might live; as a king he offered his own flesh to save a dove; as a prince he gave his life so that a starving tigress and her cubs might live. The Jatakas, in short, dramatically express the actions, in the world, of one liberated from all self-concern. They demonstrate the natural workings of the Bodhisattva mind and heart, and by so doing, turn all of existence into a vast field of spiritual effort in which no life form, no matter how seemingly insignificant, is outside the Path. All beings are revealed as potential Buddhas and Bodhisattvas. Microbe, sparrow, dog, monkey, horse, dolphin, man. Each at its own level can feel compassion for the suffering of others and act selflessly to ease the pain of all beings. At some moment in life, it seems, each is offered an opportunity and a choice. Besides revealing the character of the Buddha in his own Path to Buddhahood, the Jatakas simultaneously validate and give credence to our own natural feelings of compassion and our own spontaneous acts of selflessness. These tales ideally show us how to live in a suffering world, as well as offer us a noble and deeply spiritual vision of the nature of the universe.

The message of the Jatakas is especially poignant in our own time. As we grow increasingly aware of the depredations our own twentieth century lifestyles make on the planet, as the plight of whales, mountain gorillas, wolves, and other endangered species, as well as the cruel treatment which cats, dogs, rabbits, monkeys, rats, and mice receive—often to little purpose—in our laboratories, becomes increasingly clear to us, the Jatakas can only stand out in even greater relief. Who knows, perhaps, as the Jatakas suggest, among the very animals which we as a culture now maim, torment, slaughter, and devour are sensitive and aspiring beings, Bodhisattvas and future Buddhas. The Jatakas, once taken to heart, transform our own sensibilities and imaginations. After entering the world of the Jatakas, it becomes impossible not to feel more deeply for animals. It also becomes harder to believe that they are simply "below us"—that they are here for our own enjoyment and use. The Jatakas help us sense that animals have their own lives, their own karma, tests, purposes, and aspirations. And, as often brief and painful as their lives may be, they are also graced with a purity and a clarity which we can only humbly respect, and perhaps even occasionally envy. The Jatakas validate our deepest feelings and keep alive for us today knowledge of the wisdom inherent in all life forms. To lose respect for other species and the fundamental wisdom they too embody is, after all, to weaken the first and most fundamental of the precepts—not to kill but to cherish all life. Was not the Buddha a hare? a quail? a monkey, a lion, deer or ox? Who is to say that the dog guarding our porch or the cat twining around our legs is not a Bodhisattva on the Path even now? Entering the market one sees live rabbits and chickens and turkeys for sale. And one wonders, "Why are they here?" and is torn. "Should I buy them all? How can I save them?" For in the Jatakas one has seen that their inner life is the same as our own. One seeks to save them all, and they too, looking out at us with black or with golden shining eyes, yearn only to liberate us.

Let me tell you a classic Jataka tale:

THE HUNGRY TIGRESS

Once, long, long ago, the Buddha came to life as a noble prince named Mahasattva, in a land where the country of Nepal exists today. One day, when he was grown, he went walking in a wild forest with his two older brothers. The sky seemed alight with flames.

Suddenly, they saw a tigress. The brothers turned to flee, but the tigress stumbled and fell. She was starving and desperate and her two cubs were starving too. She eyed her cubs miserably and, in that dark glance, the prince sensed long months of hunger and pain. He saw too that unless she had food soon, she might even be driven to devour her own cubs. He was moved by compassion for the difficulty of their lives. "What, after all, is this life for?" he thought.

Stepping forward, he removed his outer garments and lay down before her. Tearing his skin with a stone, he let the starving tigress smell the blood. Mahasattva's brothers fled. Hungrily, the tigress devoured the prince's body and chewed the bones. She and her cubs lived on, and for many years the forest was filled with a golden light.

Centuries later, a mighty king raised a pillar of carved stone on this spot, and pilgrims still go there to make offerings even today.

Deeds of Compassion live on forever.

In this powerful and mysterious story, deep compassion, that profound, spontaneous inner urge to help others, is clearly and unhesitatingly embodied. Does the story mean that we too, as Buddhists, should rush out and open our veins so that starving dogs and cats may live? Perhaps for someone in whom such a response arose unself-consciously, with no need to imitate or prove a thing, that would be the Way. But for most of us, this Jataka and others like it imaginatively sustain our own vision of the real nature of things, and pose fundamental questions which can only be resolved, over time, through the daily realities of our own practice and lives. Jatakas like "The Hungry Tigress" acknowledge our inter-relation with all living things. And they remind us that, at some point, we too must act on our own deepest intuitions and experiences.

Compassion, they seem to say, must ultimately express itself in action, must take form, if it is to be real. How one does this, of course, is up to each of us. There is no one "right" way. All sincere efforts will be equally to the point.

Working with others to create communities that liberate the best in all their members; working selflessly to bring an end to the hells of nuclear destruction; creating places and opportuni-

ties for practice and teaching; caring for the land itself and for
the many species which share its bounty with us; exposing the
pitiful plight of laboratory animals; working to nourish the hearts
and imaginations of children lost in a land of soulless TV
dreams—wherever one turns, the opportunities are present. The
tigress is before our eyes.

Such activities are part of the cutting of firewood and the
drawing of water for today's world. The modern world of engaged Buddhism, the traditional world of the Jatakas and of the
Bodhisattva Path, and the confusing, fragmented world in which
we daily live and work today are, after all, seamlessly connected
can cannot be separated from one another by even so much as
the thickness of a single whisker or hair.

WALPOLA RAHULA

The Social Teachings of the Buddha

The common belief that to follow the Buddha's teaching one has to retire from life is a misconception. It is really an unconscious defense against practicing it. There are numerous references in Buddhist literature to men and women living ordinary, normal family lives who successfully practiced what the Buddha taught, and realized Nirvana. Vacchogatta the Wanderer once asked the Buddha straightforwardly whether there were laymen and women leading the family life, who followed his teaching successfully and attained to high spiritual states. The Buddha categorically stated that there were not one or two, not a hundred or two hundred or five hundred, but many more laymen and women leading the family life who followed his teaching successfully and attained to high spiritual states.[1]

It may be agreeable for certain people to live a retired life in a quiet place away from noise and disturbance. But it is certainly more praiseworthy and courageous to practice Buddhism living among your fellow beings, helping them and being of service to them. It may perhaps be useful in some cases for a person to live in retirement for a time in order to improve his or her mind and character, as preliminary moral, spiritual, and intellectual training, to be strong enough to come out later and help others. But if someone lives an entire life in solitude, thinking only of their own happiness and salvation, without caring for their fellow beings, this surely is not in keeping with the Buddha's teaching which is based on love, compassion, and service to others.

Those who think that Buddhism is interested only in lofty ideals, high moral and philosophical thought, and that it ignores the social and economic welfare of people, are wrong. The Buddha was interested in the happiness of people. To him happiness was not possible without leading a pure life based on moral and spiritual principles. But he knew that leading such a life was hard in unfavorable material and social conditions.

Buddhism does not consider material welfare as an end in itself: it is only a means to an end—a higher and nobler end. But it is a means which is indispensable, indispensable in achieving a higher purpose for human happiness. So Buddhism recognizes the need of certain minimum material conditions favorable to spiritual success—even that of a monk engaged in meditation in some solitary place.[2]

The Buddha did not take life out of the context of its social and economic background; he looked at it as a whole, in all its social, economic, and political aspects. His teachings on ethical, spiritual, and philosophical problems are fairly well known. But little is known, particularly in the West, about his teaching on social, economic, and political matters. Yet there are numerous discourses dealing with these scattered throughout the ancient Buddhist texts. Let us take only a few examples.

The *Cakkavattisihanada-sutta* of the *Digha-nikaya*[3] clearly states that poverty (*daliddiya*) is the cause of immorality and crimes such as theft, falsehood, violence, hatred, cruelty, etc. Kings in ancient times, like governments today, tried to suppress crime through punishment. The *Kutadanta-sutta* of the same *Nikaya* explains how futile this is. It says that this method can never be successful. Instead the Buddha suggests that, in order to eradicate crime, the economic condition of the people should be improved: grain and other facilities for agriculture should be provided for farmers and cultivators; capital should be provided for traders and those who are engaged in business; adequate wages should be paid to those

who are employed. When people are thus provided for with opportunities for earning a sufficient income, they will be contented, will have no fear or anxiety, and consequently the country
will be peaceful and free from crime.

Because of this, the Buddha told laypeople how important it is
to improve their economic condition. This does not mean that he
approved of hoarding wealth with desire and attachment, which
is against his fundamental teaching, nor did he approve of each
and every way of earning one's livelihood. There are certain
trades like the production and sale of armaments, which he
condemns as evil means of livelihood.

A man named Dighajanu once visited the Buddha and said:
"Venerable Sir, we are ordinary laymen, leading the family life
with wife and children. Would the Blessed One teach us some
doctrines which will be conducive to our happiness in this
world and hereafter."

The Buddha tells him that there are four things which are
conducive to a man's happiness in this world: First: he should be
skilled, efficient, earnest, and energetic in whatever profession
he is engaged, and he should know it well (utthana-sampada);
second: he should protect his income, which he has thus earned
righteously, with the sweat of his brow (arakkha-sampada); (This
refers to protecting wealth from thieves, etc. All these ideas
should be considered against the background of the period);
third: he should have good friends (kalyana-mitta) who are faith-
ful, learned, virtuous, liberal, and intelligent, who will help him
along the right path away from evil; fourth: he should spend rea-
sonably, in proportion to his income, neither too much nor too
little, i.e., he should not hoard wealth avariciously, nor should he
be extravagant—in other words he should live within his means
(samajivikata).

Then the Buddha expounds the four virtues conducive to a
layman's happiness hereafter: Saddha - He should have faith and
confidence in moral, spiritual, and intellectual values. Sila - He
should abstain from destroying and harming life, from stealing
and cheating, from adultery, from falsehood, and from intoxicating drinks. Caga - He should practice charity, generosity,

without attachment and craving for his wealth. *Pañña* - He should develop wisdom which leads to the complete destruction of suffering, to the realization of Nirvana.[4]

Sometimes the Buddha even went into details about saving money and spending it, as, for instance, when he told the young man Sigala that he should spend one fourth of his income on his daily expenses, invest half in his business and put aside one fourth for any emergency.[5]

Once the Buddha told Anathapindika, the great banker, one of his most devoted lay disciples who founded for him the celebrated Jetavana monastery at Savatthi, that a layman who leads an ordinary family life has four kinds of happiness. The first happiness is to enjoy economic security or sufficient wealth acquired by just and righteous means (*atthi-sukha*); the second is spending that wealth liberally on himself, his family, his friends and relatives, and on meritorious deeds (*bhoga-sukha*); the third is to be free from debts (*anana-sukha*); the fourth happiness is to live a faultless and a pure life, without committing evil in thought, word, or deed (*anavajja-sukha*). It must be noted here that three of these kinds of happiness are economic, and that the Buddha finally reminded the banker that economic and material happiness is "not worth one-sixteenth part" of the spiritual happiness arising out of a faultless and good life.[6]

From these few examples, one can see that the Buddha considered economic welfare as requisite for human happiness, but that he did not recognize progress as real and true if it was only material, devoid of a spiritual and moral foundation. While encouraging material progress, Buddhism always lays great stress on the development of the moral and spiritual character for a happy, peaceful, and contented society.

The Buddha was just as clear on politics, on war and peace. It is too well known to be repeated here that Buddhism advocates and preaches nonviolence and peace as its universal message, and does not approve of any kind of violence or destruction of life. According to Buddhism there is nothing that can be called a "just war"—which is only a false term coined and put into circulation to justify and excuse hatred, cruelty, violence, and massacre. Who decides what is just or unjust? The mighty and the victorious are "just," and the weak and the defeated are "unjust." Our war is always "just," and your war is always "unjust." Buddhism does not accept this position.

The Buddha not only taught nonviolence and peace, but he even went to the field of battle itself and intervened personally and prevented war, as in the case of the dispute between the Sakyas and the Koliyas, who were prepared to fight over the question of the waters of the Rohini. And his words once prevented King Ajatasattu from attacking the kingdom of the Vajjis.

In the days of the Buddha, as today, there were rulers who governed their countries unjustly. People were oppressed and exploited, tortured and persecuted, excessive taxes were imposed and cruel punishments were inflicted. The Buddha was deeply moved by these inhumanities. The *Dhammapadatthakatha* records that he, therefore, directed his attention to the problem of good government. His views should be appreciated against the social, economic and political background of his time. He had shown how a whole country could become corrupt, degenerate, and unhappy when the heads of its government, that is the king, the ministers, and administrative officers become corrupt and unjust. For a country to be happy it must have a just government. How this form of just government could be realized is explained by the Buddha in his teaching of the "Ten Duties of the King" (*dasa-rajadhamma*), as given in the *Jataka* text.[7]

Of course the term "king" (*Raja*) of old should be replaced today by the term "Government." "The Ten Duties of the King," therefore, apply today to all those who constitute the government, such as the head of state, ministers, political leaders, legislative and administrative officers, etc.

The first of the "Ten Duties of the King" is liberality, generosity, charity (*dana*). The ruler should not have craving and attachment to wealth and property, but should give it away for the welfare of the people.

Second: A high moral character (sila). He should never destroy life, cheat, steal and exploit others, commit adultery, utter falsehood, and take intoxicating drinks. That is, he must at least observe the Five Precepts (Panca-sila), the minimum moral obligations of a lay Buddhist—(1) not to destroy life, (2) not to steal, (3) not to commit adultery, (4) not to tell lies, (5) not to take intoxicating drinks.

Third: Sacrificing everything for the good of the people (pariccaga), he must be prepared to give up all personal comfort, name and fame, and even his life, in the interest of the people.

Fourth: Honesty and integrity (ajjava). He must be free from fear or favor in the discharge of his duties, must be sincere in his intentions, and must not deceive the public.

Fifth: Kindness and gentleness (maddava). He must possess a genial temperament.

Sixth: Austerity in habits (tapa). He must lead a simple life, and should not indulge in a life of luxury. He must have self-control.

Seventh: Freedom from hatred, ill-will, enmity (akkodha). He should bear no grudge against anybody.

Eighth: Nonviolence (avihimsa), which means not only that he should harm nobody, but also that he should try to promote peace by avoiding and preventing war, and everything which involves violence and destruction of life.

Ninth: Patience, forbearance, tolerance, understanding (khanti). He must be able to bear hardships, difficulties and insults without losing his temper.

Tenth: Non-opposition, non-obstruction (avirodha), that is to say that he should not oppose the will of the people, should not obstruct any measures that are conducive to the welfare of the people. In other words he should rule in harmony with his people.[8]

The Buddha says: "Never by hatred is hatred appeased, but it is appeased by kindness. This is an eternal truth."[9] "One should win anger through kindness, wickedness through goodness, selfishness through charity, and falsehood through truthfulness."[10]

There can be no peace or happiness for a man as long as he desires and thirsts after conquering and subjugating his neighbor. As the Buddha says: "The victor breeds hatred, and the defeated lies down in misery. He who renounces both victory and defeat is happy and peaceful."[11] The only conquest that brings peace and happiness is self-conquest. "One may conquer millions in battle, but he who conquers himself, only one, is the greatest of conquerors."[12]

Buddhism aims at creating a society where the ruinous struggle for power is renounced; where calm and peace prevail away from conquest and defeat; where the persecution of the innocent is vehemently denounced; where one who conquers oneself is more respected than those who conquer millions by military and economic warfare; where hatred is conquered by kindness, and evil by goodness; where enmity, jealously, ill-will and greed do not infect men's minds; where compassion is the driving force of action; where all, including the least of living things, are treated with fairness, consideration and love; where life in peace and harmony, in a world of material contentment, is directed towards the highest and noblest aim, the realization of the Ultimate Truth, Nirvana.

NOTES

[1]*Majjhima-nikaya*, I (Pali Text Society edition), pp. 30-31.

[2]*Majjhima-nikayatthakatha, Papancasudani*, I (Pali Text Society), p. 290 ff. Buddhist monks, members of the order of the *Sangha*, are not expected to have personal property, but they are allowed to hold communal (*Sanghika*) property.

[3]No. 26.

[4]*Anguttara-nikaya*, ed. Devamitta Thera (Colombo, 1929) and Pali Text Society, pp. 786 ff.

[5]*Digha-nikaya*, III, ed. Nanavasa Thera (Colombo, 1929), p. 115.

[6]*Anguttara-nikaya*, ed. Davamitta Thera (Colombo, 1929) and Pali Text Society edition, pp. 232-233.

[7]Jataka I, 260, 399; II, 400, 274, 320; V, 119, 378.

[8]It is interesting to note here that the Five Principles or *Pancha-sila* in India's foreign policy are in accordance with the Buddhist principles which Asoka, the great Buddhist emperor of India, applied to the administration of his government in the 3rd century B.C.E. The expression *Pancha-sila* (Five Precepts or Virtues), is itself a Buddhist term.

[9]*Dhammapada*, ed. K. Khammaratana Thera (Colombo, 1926), I 5.

[10]*Ibid.* XVII 3.

[11]*Ibid.* XV 5.

[12]*Ibid* VIII 4.

ROBERT A. F. THURMAN

Edicts of Asoka

The Edicts of Asoka, the third century B.C.E. rock-carved records of the practical measures taken by India's greatest emperor, should provide the operative principles of the "politics of enlightenment," to which Asoka gave the first large scale political implementation. It is perhaps most convenient and memorable to sort the passages under five headings: transcendentalism, nonviolence, religious pluralism with educational emphasis, compassionate welfare policy, and an intriguing combination of a powerful central authority implementing decentralist moves.

1. TRANSCENDENTALISM

Rock Edict XIII: The Kalinga country was conquered by King Priyadarsi in the eighth year of his reign. One hundred fifty thousand persons were carried away captive, one hundred thousand were slain, and many times that number died. Immediately after the Kalingas had been conquered, King Priyadarsi became intensely devoted to the study of Dharma, to the love of Dharma, and to the inculcation of Dharma. The Beloved of the Gods, conqueror of the Kalingas, is moved to remorse now. For he has felt profound sorrow and regret because the conquest of a people previously unconquered involved slaughter, death, and deportation....Thus all men share in the misfortune, and this weighs on King Priyadarsi's mind....King Priyadarsi now thinks that even a person who wrongs him must be forgiven for wrongs that can be forgiven,....seeks to induce even the forest people who have come under his dominion to adopt this way of life and this ideal,...desires security, self control, impartiality, and cheerfulness for all living creatures....King Priyadarsi considers moral conquest (*Dharmavijaya*) the most important conquest. He has achieved this moral conquest repeatedly both here and among the people living beyond the borders of his kingdom, even as far away as six hundred *yojanas* (3000 miles), where the Yona king Antiyoka rules (Antiochus II Theos of Syria, 261-246), and even beyond Antiyoka in the realms of the four kings named Turamaya (Ptolemy II Philadelphos 285-247), Antikini (Antigonos Gonatos of Macedonia 278-239), Maba (Magas of Cyrene 300-258), and Alikasudara (Alexander of Epirus 272-258), and to the south among the Cholas and the Pandyas....Wherever conquest is achieved by Dharma, it produces satisfaction. Satisfaction is firmly established by conquest by Dharma. Even satisfaction, however, is of little importance. King Priyadarsi attaches value ultimately only to consequences of action in the other world (future life)....This is good, here and hereafter. Let their pleasure be pleasure in Dharma (*Dharmarati*). For this alone is good, here and hereafter.

This edict records Asoka's conversion, his elevation of transcendent values above mundane goals of aggrandizement, satisfaction, and so forth. A rare case even today of a ruler admitting the wrongness of his acts and policies, and this a ruler at the height of his power, not under any pressure. Pillar Edict I goes on to describe the same principles as governing his administration:

It is difficult to achieve happiness, either in this world or the next, except by intense love of Dharma, intense self-examination, intense obedience, intense fear of sin, and intense enthusiasm. Yet as a result of my instruction, regard for Dharma and love of Dharma have increased day by day and will continue to increase. My officials of all ranks—high, low, and intermediate—act in accord with the precepts of my instruction, and by their example and influence they are able to recall fickle-minded people to their duty....For these are their rules: to govern according to the Dharma, to administer justice according to the Dharma, to advance the people's happiness according to the Dharma, and to protect them according to the Dharma.

2. NONVIOLENCE

Asoka's insistence on nonviolence is well established, as in Rock Edict IV:

> For many hundred years in the past, slaughter of animals, cruelty to living creatures, discourtesy to relatives, and disrespect for priests and ascetics have been increasing. But now because of King Priyadarsi's practice of the Dharma, the sound of war-drums has become the call to Dharma, summoning the people to exhibitions of the chariots of the gods, elephants, fireworks, and other heavenly displays. King Priyadarsi's inculcation of Dharma has increased, beyond anything observed in many hundreds of years: abstention from killing animals and from cruelty to living beings, kindliness in human and family relations, respect for priests and ascetics, and obedience to mother and father and elders....

Note how nonviolence to animals and humans is linked. Not that Asoka was able to create an instant Buddha-land. Far from it; he even had to retain the death penalty, in extreme cases, although he instituted an appeal procedure. Pillar Edict V has a long list of various species of animals under his protection, hunting bans, and so forth. And Rock Edict I records his own quite human struggle to overcome an addiction to meat eating. After prohibiting sacrificial feasts:

> Many hundreds of living creatures were formerly slaughtered every day for the curries in the kitchens of His Majesty. At present, when this Edict on Dharma is being inscribed, only three living creatures are killed daily: two peacocks and a deer, and the deer is not slaughtered regularly. In the future, not even these three animals shall be slaughtered....

India today has more widespread vegetarianism than any other country in the world, and, although Buddhism supposedly disappeared there some centuries ago, this is the first evidence of such practices on any scale, this under a Buddhist king.

3. RELIGIOUS PLURALISM AND EMPHASIS ON EDUCATION

The Maski Rock Edict proclaims Asoka's own personal practice of Buddhism:

> For more than two and a half years, I have been a lay disciple (*upasaka*) of the Buddha. More than a year ago, I attended upon the Samgha, and since then I have been energetic in my efforts....

On the Bhabra Rock Edict, he further addresses the Samgha:

> King Priyadarsi of Magadha conveys his greetings to the Samgha and wishes them good health and prosperity. You know, Reverend Sirs, the extent of my reverence for and faith in the Buddha, the Dharma, and the Samgha. Whatever the Lord Buddha has said, Reverend Sirs, is of course well said....

However, in spite of his own allegiance to Buddhism and reverence for the mendicants, he still instructs them about not engaging in sectarianism, called "Community-dissension" (*Samghabheda*), and he encourages them to read certain practical texts and make progress in their own attainments.

Of extreme interest here is his restraint in not identifying his own religion as a state religion. The transcendent Dharma is yet imminent everywhere and paramount in all activities, but no religious order is exclusively upheld—thus separation of church and state. Pillar Edict CII records this:

> My officers charged with the spread of Dharma are occupied with various kinds of services beneficial to ascetics and householders, and they are empowered to concern themselves with all sects. I have ordered some of them to look after the affairs of the Samgha

(Buddhist), some to take care of the Brahmin and Ajivika ascetics, some to work among the Nigranthas (Jaina), and some among the various other religious sects. Different officials are thus assigned specifically to the affairs of different religions, but my officers for spreading Dharma are occupied with all sects.

His clear distinction between a "religion" (*desana*) and the Dharma, as a universal moral norm or transcendent Truth, is most instructive and is indeed the invariable, solid metaphysical basis for the policy of separation of church and state, as it ensures that people always remember that the transcendent can never be encapsulated in any formula, doctrine, or behavioral, legalistic orthodoxy, but can only be embodied in a virtuous way of life. He makes this even more clear in Rock Edicts VII and XII:

> King Priyadarsi wishes members of all faiths to live everywhere in his kingdom; for they all seek mastery of the senses and purity of mind. Men are different in their inclinations and passions, however, and they may perform the whole of their duties or only part. Even if one is not able to make lavish gifts, mastery of the senses, purity of mind, gratitude, and steadfast devotion are commendable and essential....King Priyadarsi honors men of all faiths, members of religious orders and laymen alike, with gifts and various marks of esteem. Yet he does not value either gifts or honors as much as growth in the qualities essential to religion in men of all faiths. This growth may take many forms, but its root is in guarding one's speech to avoid extolling one's own faith and disparaging the faith of others improperly, or, when the occasion is appropriate, immoderately. The faiths of others all deserve to be honored for one reason or another. By honoring them, one exalts one's own faith and at the same time performs a service to the faith of others....Therefore concord alone is commendable; for through concord, men may learn and respect the conception of Dharma accepted by others. King Priyadarsi desires men of all faiths to know each other's doctrines and to acquire sound doctrines....The objective of these measures is the promotion of each man's particular faith and the glorification of the Dharma.

(Now and then, I think it wakes us up to remember that these edicts were promulgated in the third century B.C.E.!)

Asoka never forgets further that actual practice is the essence, as in Pillar Edict VII:

> The people can be induced to advance in Dharma by only two means, by moral prescriptions and by meditation (*bhavana*, which can be translated equally well as "practice" or even "realization," hence not to be understood merely as quietistic meditation, but also as the cultivation of particular emotions, abilities, and predilections.) Of the two, moral prescriptions are of little consequence, but meditation is of great importance. The moral prescriptions I have promulgated include rules making certain animals inviolable, and many others. But even in the case of abstention from injuring and from killing living creatures, it is by meditation practice that people have progressed in the Dharma most.

Finally in regard to education, Rock Edict XI:

> There is no gift that can equal the gift of Dharma, the establishment of human relations on Dharma, the distribution of wealth through Dharma, or kinship in Dharma.

4. COMPASSIONATE WELFARE POLICY

Here I need not read the edicts, but merely list his activities of traveling around giving gifts extensively, commissioning his queens and ministers to do likewise, building rest-houses and hospices for the poor and sick, patronizing medicine, importing doctors and herbs from as far away as Greece, providing for convicts and their families, sending out special ministers to investigate cases of judicial harshness or corruption, freeing prisoners 25 times on holidays, and so on, generally acting as a father to his children towards all the people. An interesting point here is his treatment of all people as equals (in spite of the entrenched caste system he had to contend with) which is the only way to make sense of the enigmatic Maski Edict:

...In Jambudvipa, the gods who formerly had no relations with men have now been associated with them. But this result which I have achieved is within the power even of a poor man if he is devoted to Dharma. It is incorrect to suppose that it is limited to the rich. Poor and rich should be told, 'If you act in this way, this praiseworthy achievement will endure a long time and will be augmented at a time and a half.

Asoka here is saying that all men of all classes can be as gods by virtue of their embodiment of Dharma in kindliness, truthfulness, and so forth. It is a demand to live up to transcendent values and not pretend they are possible only in a separate realm of gods. These welfare activities of Asoka are all the more remarkable if one reads Kautilya's *Arthashastra*, written in the time of Asoka's grandfather, wherein the harshest measures of oppression are systematically and thoroughly worked out, including plans for the most effective secret police operation imaginable. As for deciding on whether it is all mere rhetoric, one can compare Megasthenes' accounts of India before Asoka with the Chinese pilgrims' detailed accounts of their travels some centuries later, and it is like night and day as far as humanistic government is concerned.

5. MONARCHIAL DECENTRALIZATION

Asoka seems to have been as busy, even overworked, as any executive today. His Rock Edicts VI and VIII give some sense of his own life-style:

In the past, state business was not transacted or reports made at all hours of the day. I have therefore made arrangements that officials may have access to me and may report on the affairs of my people at all times and in all places—when I am eating, when I am in the harem or my inner apartments, when I am attending to the cattle, when I am walking or engaged in religious exercises. I now attend to the affairs of the people in all places. And when a donation or a proclamation that I have ordered verbally, or an urgent matter which

I have delegated to my high officials, causes a debate or dispute in the Council, this must be reported to me immediately, at all hours and in all places. These are my orders. I am never completely satisfied with my work or my vigilance in carrying out public affairs. I consider the promotion of the people's welfare my highest duty, and its exercise is grounded in work and constant application. No task is more important to me than promoting the well-being of the people. Such work as I accomplish contributes to discharging the debt I owe to all living creatures to make them happy in this world and to help them attain heaven in the next....

How extraordinary for candor, dedication, and the theoretical underpinnings of a ruler's sense of debt to the people, rather than arrogance of high status, and so on, and all in the third century B.C.E.

King Priyadarsi does not consider glory or renown of great value except insofar as the people, at present and in the future, hear of his practice of the Dharma and (themselves) live in accordance with the Dharma....For this purpose he desires glory and fame." And this poor executive can't even get a vacation! "In the past kings used to go on pleasure tours. On these tours, they hunted and indulged in other pastimes. King Priyadarsi, however, became enlightened in wisdom (sambuddha) ten years after his coronation. Since then his tours have been Dharma-tours. He visits priests and ascetics and makes gifts to them; he visits the aged and gives them money; he visits the people of rural areas, instructing them in the Dharma and discussing it with them...takes great pleasure in these.

At the same time as exercising this strong authority, Asoka gave considerable autonomy to his provincial governors (Rajuka), not to be done lightly in those days, as such were always the overthrowers of central regimes, drawing on provincial garrisons and tax bases. But Asoka renounced the use of oppressive measures, such as Kautilya had so specifically detailed for his grandfather, to keep the provinces in tight subjugation, and rather relied on the welfare and educational activities of his Dharmamahamatras to grant the populace enough of a stake in his regime to maintain it. He has been greatly criticized for the looseness of his administration, which precisely kept the empire from lasting more than a couple of generations after him. But from a more modern point of view, where dominance of culture, prevalence of life-style, is more important in the long run than ubiquity of administration, we need not fault him for this. Indeed, he may very well have only been realistically accepting the prohibitive cost of keeping such a huge, populous, wealthy, diverse society under tight control. And as far as his "failure" that modern, nationalistic scholars have complained about, how can we say that his "Truth Conquest" (*Dharmavijaya*) failed, when, without military expansion at all, all of Asia accepted and put into practice the Dharma as best they could over the next millennium, and India became the Holy Land *par excellence* for all of these otherwise highly tribalistic and chauvinistic peoples?

In sum, while from the short-term nationalistic point of view, the politics of enlightenment were deficient in that Asoka passed up the chance for world-conquest, leaving the way open for the Han Chinese, Romans, and Sassanids, and although Europe did conquer India finally rather than the other way around, the game of evolution is not yet over. In a trans-national planet, such as we must surely have within decades, there will be no ancient ruler other than Asoka to point to as visionary predecessor of the rule of Dharma replacing the rule of force. It is curious how Gandhi rediscovered Asoka, a Buddhist king, rather than any of the Guptas or Phalas!

ROBERT A. F. THURMAN

Nagarjuna's Guidelines
for Buddhist Social Action

[O King!] Just as you love to consider
What to do to help yourself,
So should you love to consider
What to do to help others![1]

GREAT COMPASSION

Nargarjuna thus expresses the basic principle of Buddhist social action: the universal altruism of "great love" (mahamaitri) and "great compassion," or "great empathy" (mahakaruna). The primary Buddhist position on social action is one of total activism, an unswerving commitment to complete self-transformation and complete world-transformation. This activism becomes fully explicit in the Universal Vehicle (Mahayana),[2] with its magnificent literature on the Bodhisattva career. But it is also compellingly implicit in the Individual Vehicle (Hinayana) in both the Buddha's actions and his teachings: granted, his attention in the latter was on self-transformation, the prerequisite of social transformation. Thus, it is squarely in the center of all Buddhist traditions to bring basic principles to bear on actual contemporary problems to develop ethical, even political, guidelines for action.

This is just what Nagarjuna did during the second century C.E., when he wrote his *Jewel Garland of Royal Counsels* to his friend and disciple, King Udayi of the powerful Satavahana dynasty of south central India. It should thus prove instructive to examine his counsels in some detail. In this essay, I will sketch the Buddhist view of absolute and relative realities, which has clear implications for the derivation of ethics from metaphysics. Then I will sift through Nagarjuna's general counsels on social policy to discern the main outlines of the society he prescribed for that time and place. Finally, I will extrapolate from his specific prescriptions a set of modern "counsels" for today's "kings," in hopes that it will help the buddhistic intellectual clarify his or her own thinking about the emergencies that beset us.

TRANSCENDENT SELFLESSNESS

Nagarjuna begins the book on the transcendentalist plane, instructing the King in what he needs to know for his own liberation and self-cultivation. This is the first principle of Buddhist social ethics: individualist transcendentalism. It is most clearly expressed in the shocking advice Nagarjuna gives the King that it might be best for him to resign.

> But enlightened rule is difficult
> Due to the un-enlightenment of the world;
> So it is better you renounce the world,
> For the sake of true glory.

Such advice flies in the face of all worldly political wisdom, ancient or modern, but it is at the heart of Buddhist politics and ethics. The "sacred duty" of the king, the "supreme responsibility" of the President, (i.e., the sacred pompousness of rulers) all derive from the idea that the will and the necessity of the collective are supreme over those of the individual. The prime self-sacrificer is thus supposed to be the ruler himself or herself. "Heavy lies the head that wears the crown..." and so forth, the idea is well-known. The king must put the collective ahead of himself, submerge his individual interest in the collective interest, and his so doing confirms that all individuals in the society matter less than the collective "people." This is the essence of collectivism and secularism, and is the same in any totalitarian state, whether fascist, communist, monarchical/imperialist, whatever. Against this Nagarjuna proclaims the supremacy of the individual, starting with the king himself, more importantly a human being than a social role, even the most important social role. The best thing the king can do for his nation is, finally, to perfect himself. The best use of his own "precious jewel of a human life endowed with leisure and opportunity" is to attain his own enlightenment, for which purpose he may renounce the world and enter the monastic discipline of spiritual virtuosity.

The practical impact of this advice is that the necessities and will of the collective, the "business of society," is just not that important. It is, after all, made up of individuals; their collective interest is the specific sum of their individual interests, one by one. Therefore, as the enlightenment of each one individually is the most important thing for each one, one by one, the enlightenment of any one individual is of supreme importance at any one time.

The fundamental importance of individualist transcendentalism is witnessed by the fact that more than two-thirds of the *Counsels* contain personal instructions on the core insight of individualism, namely subjective and objective selflessnesses.[3] This type of instruction is called the teaching of "transcendence" (*nihsreyasa*), the summum bonum. Based on these, though leading beginners up to them, are the teachings of "ascendance" (abhyudaya), methods to improve one's status and ability in the world. Ascendance teachings call for faith, mainly; transcendence teachings call for wisdom. Ascendance teachings are summarized early in the *Counsels*.

Here are given the Buddhist "Commandments," "not to kill, not to take the not given, not to rape, not to lie, abuse, slander, or gossip, not to bear envy, malice, or false convictions;" matched by injunctions to "prolong life, give gifts, maintain proper sexuality, tell the truth, reconcile conflicts, speak gently, speak meaningfully, be loving, rejoice in others' fortune, hold authentic views." Following this ten-fold path of virtuous evolution,[4] one "ascends" in the stations of worldly life, being reborn in human and divine realms.

Next, and in much more detail, Nagarjuna turns to the transcendence teachings.

> The teachings of transcendence
> The Victors call profound,
> Subtle and terrifying to the unlearned immature.

He begins transcendence teaching by demonstrating the un-
reality of the "I"-notion. The king should first be aware that his "I"
and his "mine" are illusory, not established in reality as they habitually appear to be.

> "I am," and "It is mine,"
> These are false as absolutes,
> For neither stands existent
> Under exact knowledge of reality.
>
> The "I"-habit creates the heaps,
> Which "I"-habit is false in fact.
> How can what grows from a false seed
> Itself be truly existent?
>
> Having seen the heaps as unreal,
> The "I"-habit is abandoned.
> "I"-habit abandoned, the heaps do not arise again.

With characteristic boldness, Nagarjuna's first transcendent
teaching to the King is that " 'you' and 'yours' do not really exist
the way 'you' think they do"! The previous ascendance teaching
leaves the King's self-image intact, admonishing him to be good,
by not killing, not taking what is not given, and so forth. But
transcendence begins with the discarding of the self-image, and
it aims for liberation, beyond good and evil. This evinces the
same emphasis on attitude and wisdom that also puts authentic
view (*samyakdrsti*) as the first of the eight components of the path.
The world arises from the delusions "I am" and "I have," but since
they are delusions, notwithstanding scientific investigation, the
world itself is delusory in nature. Thus by terminating the delu-

sions, the world of suffering is terminated, the world of the compulsive heaps (*skandha*). Thus, the world-creator, the root of all evil, is this "I"-habit, this fundamental misknowledge. And the root of good, of positive social action is the individual's realization of this subjective selflessness.

However, this absolute non-existence of the self does not itself exist as an absolute self of non-existence, such as the Ajivikas, Carvakas, and other Indian negativistic thinkers supposed. Just as the world only exists relatively, in an illusory way, so the "transcendent," the "beyond," is also only illusory. "Nirvana" only has meaning as opposite of "samsara." Terminate the one and the other is also obsolete. Therefore, liberation is not just an easy non-existence. "If nirvana is not a nothing, just how could it be something? The termination of the misconceptions of things and non-things is called Nirvana."

Furthermore, "Because in reality there is no coming, going, or staying, what ultimate difference is there between the world and Nirvana?...Ultimately the world cannot through Nirvana disappear." Such is the accurate intuition of the uncreated nature of reality, the non-duality of absolute and relative, the objective selflessness and the subjective selflessness. This intuition can be expanded limitlessly by the scientific procedures of critical wisdom until virtual omniscience is attained. Sparing no technical detail, Nagarjuna sets forth the full picture of transcendence for King Udayi, and he affirms the non-duality of the bodhisattva way by demanding that such wisdom be attained by the King himself: "From wisdom comes a mind unshakeable, relying not on others, firm and not deceived. therefore, O King, be intent on wisdom." Social reality is not a lesser sphere, to be taken care of by those incapable of enlightenment. Each one, even political managers, must themselves achieve their own independent individual enlightenment.

One might wonder why, in such a letter of counsels, Nagarjuna spends such a long time on first principles, on analysis of earth, air, fire, water, and consciousness, on refutation of being and nothingness, on transcendence of unity and plurality. He could simply have referred the King to his classic *Wisdom*, the exhaustive unpacking of the subject, with its accompanying *Emptiness Seventy, Counter-Rebuttal*, and *Philosophical Sixty*.[5] But it is clearly in keeping with the principle of individualist transcendentalism that the bodhisattva person of action can and must be responsible for intuitive wisdom, and so he presents the king with a quintessence of the methods for developing the wisdom-basis of effective social action.

Furthermore, this is Nagarjuna's own way of practicing what he preaches. He does not consider any ends of society, achieved by getting the king to follow his policies, to be as important as the king's own self-development and self-liberation. A liberated and compassionate king will himself choose the right path of action and be more effective than a merely obedient, unliberated king who must depend slavishly on Nagarjuna's or someone else's ideas.

In sum, the fact that the majority of the *Garland* is devoted to the transcendent selflessness, the door of the liberation and enlightenment of the individual, is clear evidence that the heart of Buddhist social activism is individualistic transcendentalism. The attainment of Nirvana is everyone's Ultimate Good, and the good of each single person is always more important than any good of any putative whole or collective. Thus, the Individual Vehicle, the Buddha's "original" teaching, remains indispensable, the essence of the Universal Vehicle as well.[6]

DETACHMENT

The second major strand in Nagarjuna's *Counsels* is that of self-restraint, unpacked as detachment and pacifism. The king will not be able to act selflessly without the basis of intuitive wisdom which understands the critique of the "I" and the "objective self," realizing their ultimate non-existence and conventional relativity. Likewise, he will not be able to resist the temptations of consumption, food, possessions, sex, if he does not understand the reality of the objects of his passions. Therefore Nagarjuna dwells extensively on the time-worn and effective meditation on ugliness (*asubhatva*) to help the king free himself from passion.

He realized that it is not easy to change long-standing preferences and habits of attachment, nor is it pleasant to scrutinize long-loved objects under the harsh light of critical analysis. So he carefully prefaces his excursion into the horrific: "Rare indeed are helpful speakers. Listeners are rarer. But rarer still are words which though unpleasant help at once! Therefore, having realized the unpleasant to be helpful, act on it quickly, just as when ill, one takes even nauseating medicine from a person of concern." He immediately affirms the impermanence of life, health, and dominion. "Seeing that death is certain, and that when dead one suffers from one's sins, you should not sin, foregoing passing pleasure." He forbids the ruler drinking and gambling, and then comes to the most important, sex:

> Lust of women comes mostly from thinking that her body is clean, but there is nothing clean in a woman's body....The body is a vessel filled with excrement, urine, lungs, and liver...an ornamented pot of filth....He who lies on the filthy mass covered by skin moistened with those fluids, merely lies on top of a woman's bladder....How could the nature of this putrid corpse, a rotten mass covered by skin, not be seen when it looks so very horrible?...Since your own body is as filthy as any woman's, should you not abandon lust for self and other both?....If you yourself wash this body dripping from its nine wounds and still do not think it filthy—what use have you for profound instruction?

Nagarjuna courageously invades the royal harem, bathrooms, and even toilets, to force the king to confront the inherent unclean nature of the body in its daily functions, in its putrefaction and death, and in its biological urges. If the king will courageously confront these coarse facts: "If you thus analyze, even though you do not become free from desire, because your desire has lessened, you will no longer lust for women."

This section concludes with a warning not to hunt and kill animals, because of the unpleasantness of this for the animals and the hellish effects eventually for the hunter/killer.

The themes collected under this principle of "pacifism," namely revulsion from lusts, restraint of aggressions, vanity of possessions and power, are drawn by Nagarjuna from the basic Individual Vehicle teachings of renunciation (*pravajya*). To modern persons, they may seem to lead to a drab puritanism, a killjoy asceticism. Certainly, they are not the kind of cosmetic encouragement people of wealth and power expect to hear. And here is where Buddhist social action shows its realism, its "hardnosed" acceptance of the facts of life, grounding the heroism of transcendent virtue in the effective calmness of a deglamorized awareness.

TRANSFORMATIVE UNIVERSALISM

Next, Nagarjuna turns to the third principle of Buddhist social activism, that of transformative universalism. This is expressed specifically in the complete commitment to a pluralistic, enlightenment-oriented educational effort, considered the major business of the whole nation. His general counsel begins with the Teacher. "With respect and without stint you should construct Images of Buddha, reliquaries and temples, and provide abundant endowment,...construct images of the buddha from all precious substances." The Buddha image is not, as Westerners have assumed, merely an object of devotion. Though it has a devotional function at the most popular level, its main function is inspirational. It is meant to represent the fullest potential of all the people, to inspire them all to transform themselves and reach their own perfection of evolution. Thus the buddha is the image of each individual's own perfection. Next, "you should sustain with all your effort the Excellent Teaching, and the Monastic Community." Once the image of perfection is everywhere to act as inspiration, there are the actual teachings themselves (*Dharma*), the teachings individuals may use to develop and liberate themselves. Finally, to put these teachings into practice, teachers are required, who must also be exemplary practitioners, both of which functions were fulfilled by the monastic communities (*Samgha*). "You should make donations of Sakyamuni's Scriptures and the scientific texts based upon them, as well as of the paper, pens, and inks needed to copy them. As the strategy to increase wisdom, take regions where there are schools of letters, and assure their grants of estates to provide the livelihood of the teachers."

COMPASSIONATE SOCIALISM

The fourth principle of Buddhist activism, compassionate socialism, concerns the economic and legal administration of society. Here Nagarjuna describes the welfare state, astoundingly, millennia ahead of its time, a rule of compassionate socialism based on a psychology of abundance, achieved by generosity. "To dispel the sufferings of children, the elderly, and the sick, please fix farm revenues for doctors and barbers throughout the land." This is a concise description of a socially-supported universal health care delivery system. "Please have a kind intelligence and set up hostels, parks, canals, irrigation ponds, rest houses, wells, beds, food, grass, and firewood." A policy of total care of all citizens is plainly recommended, including care for travelers, even strangers passing through, and special shelters for beggars and cripples, and wandering ascetics. "It is not right to eat yourself until you have given seasonal food, drink, vegetables, grains, and fruits to mendicants and beggars." Nagarjuna spares no details of how these outsiders should be cared for: "Please establish rest houses in all temples, towns, and cities, and provide water fountains on arid roadways....At the fountains, place shoes, umbrellas, water filters, tweezers for removing thorns, needles, thread, and fans. Within the vessels place the three medicinal fruits, the three fever medicines, butter, honey, eye-salve, antidotes to poison, written charms, and prescriptions....Place body-salves, foot-salves, head-salves, cloth, stools, gruel, jars, pots, axes, and so forth. Please have small containers kept in shade filled with sesame, rice, grains, foods, molasses, and cool water." He even recommends a special custodian be appointed to provide food, water, sugar, and piles of grain to all anthills, caring also for dogs and birds, showing his ecological concern is wider than just for the human society.

Nagarjuna combines his social counsel with some practical economic advice. He advocates a regulated economy, with the government protecting the small farmer, that was always the basis of wealth and stability in Indian kingdoms. The royal granary should husband seed-grains against times of scarcity, taxes and tolls should be kept to a minimum. Government should control prices and release from its grain storage during bad seasons to prevent hoarding. A good police force to protect against thieves and bandits is also recommended, so one cannot accuse the *Counsels* of being altogether unrealistic.

These general counsels to the king just give him the broad outlines of an individualist, transcendentalist, pacifist, universalist, socialist society. The emphasis throughout is on the king's own self-cultivation, especially of critical wisdom (understanding selflessness and propertylessness), of detachment (understanding the questionable desirability of normal passions), universalistic love (extending the opportunity for happiness to all through education toward liberation and enlightenment), and generous compassion (dedicated to providing everyone with everything they need to satisfy their basic needs so that they may have leisure to consider their own higher needs and aims). We have very little physical evidence as to how successful King Udayi was in enacting these counsels, although the picture of the Southern kingdoms that emerges from sources like the *Avatamsaka Sutra*, the non-Sanskrit literatures of South India, the art of Ajanta and Amaravati, the accounts of the Chinese pilgrims, and the Tibetan histories is certainly idyllic. A civilization of wealthy cities, luxurious courts of great sensuous refinement, widespread scholarship and intense asceticism, prosperous farmers and peasants, relatively long-lasting peace and political stability. This picture represents a considerable advance over the India of the Mauryas, reflected in Magasthenes, the *Arthasastra*, and Asoka's Edicts.[7]

CONTEMPORARY COUNSELS

In this final section, I will turn to Nagarjuna's more detailed counsel, and I will use it as a framework on which to outline guidelines for Buddhist social action in our modern times. The fact that it is counsel to a "king" does not invalidate this approach in the least, for, as R. B. Fuller says, the average citizen of any modern, industrial or post-industrial society lives better in many ways than most kings of bygone eras; indeed is more king of his own fate than they were in many ways.[8] Therefore, everyone can apply these counsels in their own sphere of activity. Political parties could be formed with such principles in their platforms (indeed many parties do have such planks), and Buddhist communities and individuals in particular could work to spread such principles and attitudes. So, let us now read Nagarjuna as if he were addressing us today. There are 45 verses which contain the whole quintessence of the matter.[9]

Again, this section begins with some acknowledgement that good advice is often unpleasant at first hearing, especially to a rich and powerful king who is used to being flattered and having his own way. The king is urged to be tolerant of the "useful but unpleasant" words, and to consider them as true words spoken without anger and from compassion, hence fit to be heard, like water fit for bathing. "Realize that I am telling you what is useful here and later. Act on it so as to help yourself and others."

People in power are still the same. In fact, the entire populations of the "developed" countries are in a way full of people of royal powers, used to consuming what they want, being flattered and waited upon by people from "underdeveloped" lands, used to having unpleasantly realistic things such as corpses, sicknesses, madnesses, the deformities of poverty, kept out of their sight. They do not want to hear that all is impermanent, that life is essentially painful and fundamentally impure. They do not want to acknowledge that all beings are equal to them and their dear ones, equally lovable and deserving. They do not want to hear that there is no real self and no absolute property and no absolute right. But that they do hear it, and hear it well, is quite the most crucial necessity of our times. The hundreds of millions of "kings" and "queens" living in the developed world must face their obligations to other peoples, to other species, and to nature itself. This is the crisis of our times, the real one, not the supposedly important competitions among the developed "big powers."

Nagarjuna's first real statement is straight to this most crucial point. "If you do not make contributions of the wealth obtained from former giving, through such ingratitude and attachment you will not gain wealth in the future." There are two beliefs behind this simple yet far-reaching injunction to generosity, an injunction essential today. First, wealth accrues to an individual as the evolutionary effect of generosity in former lives or previously in this life. Second, wealth in this life accrues to one by the generosity of others who give to one, for whatever reason, and therefore one must be grateful to them. Bracketing the question of former lives, which is difficult for modern people, it is a fact that people who are wealthy today usually are so because previous generations worked hard and gave of themselves to the future. Capitalism itself is, in its essence, not a matter of hoarding and attachment, but a matter of ascetic self-restraint, the "investment" of wealth or the giving it up to a larger causality. The more given up from present consumption to productive investment, the more is produced for future consumption. Those who lose sight of the essence of this process and simply consume and hoard, soon lose their wealth, just as Nagarjuna states. It is a fact of economics that the basis of wealth is generosity.

Today the wealth of the modern nations comes from three main sources: (1) the generosity of hard work, self-sacrifice, and inventiveness of the former generations; (2) the generosity of older, gentler nations, from whose Asian, African, and American lands enormous wealth was exploited by western and recently westernized entrepreneurs; (3) the generosity of the earth herself, with the sun, the oceans, and the winds. Now we, the people of modern nations, must "make contributions" with that wealth to create still more wealth for the future. We can repay former generations by generosity towards future generations, by investing in their future, restraining our consumption. We can repay the heirs of the exploited by giving back some of the fruits of the wealth they let our ancestors take, especially in the form of equipment they need to produce more wealth themselves. And we can repay the earth by ceasing to pollute her, cleansing previous messes, and investing in her long-term health. We still have the chance to make these gifts voluntarily. If we fail to take it, all will inevitably be lost. Nagarjuna sums this up: "Always be of magnanimous mind, delighting in magnificent deeds. Magnanimous actions bring forth magnificent fruits."

Petty-mindedness, scarcity psychology, short-term profit seeking, destructive rapacity—these are the real enemies. Their opposite is magnanimity, which makes all people friends. In sum, transcendence is the root of generosity. Generosity is the root of evolutionary survival. Evolutionary survival eventually brings forth freedom for the bliss of transcendence. This is a golden three-strand cord more powerful than the usual heap-habit, ego-habit, addiction cycle. The former is a living Nirvana. The latter is the samsara of continual dying.

The foremost type of giving is, interestingly, not just giving of material needs, although that is a natural part of generosity. That of greatest value to beings is freedom and transcendence and enlightenment. These are obtained only through the door of Dharma, Transcendent Truth of Selflessness, Voidness, Openness, and so forth. Therefore, the educational system of a society is not there to "service" the society, to produce its drone-"professionals," its workers, its servants. The educational system is the individual's doorway to liberation, to enlightenment. It is therefore the brain of the body politic. Society has no other purpose than to foster it. It is society's door of liberation. By giving others the gift of education, they gain freedom, self-reliance, understanding, choice, all that is still summed up in the word "enlightenment." Life is for the purpose of enlightenment, not enlightenment for life. The wondrous paradox is, of course, that enlightenment makes life worthwhile: because it makes it less important, it makes it easier to give it away, whereby at last it becomes enjoyable. Therefore, human evolution is consummated in transformative education. Society becomes meaningful when it fosters education. Life is worth living when it values education supremely. And so our "royal" giving should first of all go to support universal, total, unlimited education of all individuals. Nagarjuna is very specific: "Create centers of Teaching, institutions of the Three Jewels, whose name and glory are inconceivable to lesser kings, for fear of their ill-repute after death (if they rule unwisely and selfishly)."

One reason the educational priority in Buddhist activism has been misperceived, causing Buddhists in the west, for instance, to denigrate education as "mere book-learning" or "mere intellectual time-wasting," is the mistranslation of the word "Dharma." In the verse above, where I have translated it, "Teaching" would have usually been translated either "Religion" or "Doctrine." The former term would have given the counsel a religious missionary flavor, the latter a dogmatic scholastic flavor. "Dharma" has eleven main meanings, according to Vasubandhu, ranging from "thing" to "Nirvana."[10] After "thing," it means "law," "duty," "religion," "virtue," still on the ground level, the level of preservation of order, the level of pattern-maintenance. Next, it can mean fulfillment of the "laws," and so forth. Then it can mean "Truth" as that which liberates, which makes either doctrine or teaching work. Finally, it means "path," "practice," and "Nirvana" itself, absolute reality as the goal of all the "Dharmas" in the preceding meanings, as well as their source. Thus, "Nirvana" is the subjective union with the absolute, the Dharmakaya or Dharmadhatu. Practice of the Laws, Duties, Religions, Doctrines, Teachings, Truths, or the following of the Paths they indicate, leads to that union. "Truth" is the absolute itself reflected in speech, the Word which liberates. Teachings teach the Truth, path, and practice leading to Nirvana. Doctrines predispose one to accept the Teachings by putting them into practice. Religions cause one to look in the right place for doctrines, etc., as well as preliminarily not to do anything one naturally would not do after enlightenment, and laws and duties fit with this function. finally, "qualities," "phenomena," or "things" are the patterns of ultimate reality conventionally created by our perceptual/conceptual habits.

Thus, from this clarification, we can see that Nagarjuna is not talking about merely creating "religious centers." He is not even talking about creating "Buddhist centers," "Buddhism" understood in its usual sense as one of a number of world religions. It does not matter what symbols or ideologies provide the umbrella, as long as the function is liberation and enlightenment. Clearly Nagarjuna, who proclaims repeatedly that "belief-systems," "dogmatic views," "closed convictions," "fanatic ideologies," and so forth, are sicknesses to be cured by the medicine of emptiness, is not a missionary for any particular "belief-system," even if it is labeled "Buddhism." Rather, he wants the social space filled with doorways to Nirvana, shrines of liberating Truth, facilities for Teaching and Practice, where "things," "duties," "laws," "religions," and "doctrines" can be examined, criticized, refined, used, transcended, and so forth. As already mentioned, these centers are not primarily even for the service of society, although in fact they are essential facilities for the evolutionary betterment of the people. They are the highest product of the society. As society itself has the main function of service to the individual, its highest gift to its individuals is to expose them to the transcendent potential developed by education.

Now these are institutions of the Three Jewels: the Buddha, the Dharma, and the Samgha. And, under the above, critically "de-religionized" interpretation, fully in keeping with Nagarjuna's own Centrist (*Madhyamika*) critical style, these Three Jewels can demonstrate their value without any sectarian context. In universal social terms, the Buddha is the ideal of the educated person, the full flowering of human potential, the perfectly self-fulfilled and other-fulfilling being. He/she[11] is not a god, not an object of worship, but an object of emulation, a source of enlightenment teaching. He/she is the standard of achievement. The Dharma is his/her Teaching, the Truth and Nirvana he/she realized, which all people can educate themselves to realize, as already explained. The Samgha is the Community of those dedicated to teaching and practicing this Dharma with a view of becoming and helping all become such Buddhas. Very often they are so concentrated on these tasks, they have no time for ordinary social activities, business, professions, family, and so forth, but are specialists in practice and teaching. These become mendicants, identityless, propertyless, selfless monastics, and often in Buddhist history they served as the core staff of Teaching centers. Sometimes, however, part of their Teaching and practice involved, as in the case of Vimalakirti and later the Great Adepts (*Mahasiddhas*), participation in ordinary living patterns, so it is not necessary at all times and places and at all stages of development that they observe the monastic life-style.

These institutions will gain fame, as the people come to know that they are verily the gateways to a higher order of living, a higher awareness, a fuller sensibility, a more valid knowledge. They radiate glory as the persons who have developed themselves and have transcended their previous addictive habits naturally and compassionately give invaluable assistance toward the betterment of others according to their capacities and inclinations.

In the second verse, Nagarjuna puts in an important criterion of a genuine institution of Enlightenment Teaching: it must not become a servile establishment in service of the elites of existing societies, there to provide professional training and ideological indoctrination. Its teachers and students must live transcendently, that is, valuing Truth above all personal considerations. They must thus be intensely critical of all falsehood, pretense, delusion, sham. Therefore, their sayings and writings must be so ruthlessly clear and straightforward that inferior persons, elite members as well as kings, must be terrified of being exposed in their pretenses and faults, hence inspired themselves to live and act transcendently. If the institutions are not truly liberal, i.e., liberating in this manner, they had better not be established at all.

To take Nagarjuna's counsel to heart in modern times, this means a drastic revision of our practice nowadays. Liberal education should no longer be seen as an institution necessary for the preservation and enrichment of a free society. Rather liberal education as an institution should represent the fulfillment of the very founding purpose of a free society. Kant's call for enlightenment as the "emergence from the tutelage of others" and Jefferson's call for "universal enlightenment throughout the land" should be seen as expressing the prime priority of the whole nation. Thus it is quite proper that the major expenditure in the national budget should be for education; and it should be offered free to all, regardless of class affiliation, regardless of utilitarian calculations. "If it takes all your wealth, you should disabuse the magnificent elite of their arrogance, inspire the middle classes, and refine the coarse tastes of the lowly."

Nagarjuna seems to have been aware of the economic costliness of his insistence on the priority of education, for he devotes the next five verses to persuading the king that wealth should not be hoarded for lesser necessities, and that he should go the whole way in support of higher education. He harps on the king's death, how such contributions are an investment in his future evolution, how his successor will probably waste it, how happiness comes from the generous use of wealth, not from hoarding and eventual wasting, and how, finally, if he does not do it now while he is young and in control of his ministers, they will not respect his wishes when he sees clearly on his deathbed. In his own words:

> Having let go of all possessions (at death)
> Powerless you must go elsewhere;
> But all that has been used for Dharma
> Precedes you (as positive evolutionary force).
> All the possessions of a previous King come under the control
>   of his successor.
> Of what use are they then to the previous King,
> Either for his practice, happiness, or fame?
> Through using wealth there is happiness in the here and now.
> Through giving there is happiness in the future.
> From wasting it without using it or giving it away there is
>   only misery.
> How could there be happiness?
> Because of impotence while dying,

You will be unable to make gifts through your ministers.
Shamelessly they will lose affection for you,
And will only seek to please the new King.
Therefore, now while in good health,
Create Centers of Learning with all your wealth,
For you are living amid the causes of death
Like a lamp standing in the breeze.
Also other Teaching Centers established by the previous kings,
All temples and so forth should be sustained as before.

Nagarjuna further specifies how the faculties should be chosen: "Let them be staffed by nonviolent, virtuous persons, who are truthful, firm in self-discipline, kind to visitors, tolerant, noncombative, and steadily industrious. Appoint guardians of the Teaching at all Teaching centers who are energetic, free of greed, learned, exemplary in conduct and without malice." If all our academics met this description, our institutions would be resplendent beyond imagination! Noteworthy in particular is the "exemplary" quality, insisting on a high level of embodiment in the teachers of principles taught, and not accepting our western dissociation of teaching from the personal qualities or understanding of the teacher.

From the universalism underlying the educational emphasis of Buddhist activism, Nagarjuna moves to the principle of pacifism, in specific application to the appointment of ministers, generals, officials, administration of justice, and vigilance over the actual conditions in the nation.

The choice of ministers, generals, and officials is mainly determined by whether or not they practice the Teachings, and manifest this personally by honesty, generosity, kindliness, and intelligent discrimination. Even with such people, the ruler should be in constant contact with them, and constantly admonish them to remember the overall aim and purpose of the nation: namely the Teaching, realization, and practice of the liberating Truth. "If your kingdom exists for the Truth, and not for fame, wealth, or consumption, then it will be extremely fruitful; otherwise all will finally be in vain." In modern terms, this counsel accords well with the experience of successful corporations and government administrations and agencies. They always choose their leaders from among liberally-educated persons, rather than from narrow professional circles, as it takes the special "enlightened" ability of clear critical insight to manage large complex affairs successfully.

In regard to justice, Nagarjuna tells the king to appoint elder judges, responsible, well-educated, virtuous, and pleasant persons, and even so he should intervene as much as possible to exercise compassion for criminals. "Even if they (the judges) have rightfully fined, bound or punished people, You, being softened with compassion, should still take care (of the offenders). O King, through compassion you should always generate an attitude of help, even for all beings who have committed the most appalling sins. Especially generate compassion for those murderers, whose sins are horrible; those of fallen nature are receptacles of compassion from those whose nature is great." Nagarjuna goes to the central issue concerning violence and nonviolence in a society, the issue of murder and its retribution. Taking of life is the worst violence, especially in enlightenment-valuing nations, where the precious human life, hard won by struggle up from the tormented lower forms of evolution, is the inestimably valuable stage from which most effectively to attain freedom and enlightenment. But to take a second life to avenge the first is to add violence to violence, and hence capital punishment is abolished by Nagarjuna. Punishment must be rehabilitative, and Nagarjuna's formulation of this principle may be the earliest on historical record. "As long as the prisoners are not freed (which, he says, they should be as soon as possible) they should be made comfortable with barbers, baths, food, drink, medicine, and clothing. Just as unworthy sons are punished out of a wish to make them worthy, so punishment should be enforced with compassion and not from hatred or concern for wealth. Once you have examined the fierce murderers and judged them correctly, you should banish them without killing or torturing them." The nonviolent treatment of criminals, even capital offenders, accords with every principle of Buddhist teaching: (1) compassion, of course, in that love must be extended most of all to the undeserving, the difficult to love; further, for society to kill sanctions killing indirectly, setting a bad example; (2) impermanence, in that the minds of beings are changeable, and commission of evil once does not necessarily imply a permanent habit of doing evil; (3) selflessness implies the conditionality of each act, and the reformability of any personality; (4) the preciousness and value of life, especially human life.

In modern times, it is to the great credit of those modern societies founded on enlightenment principles that they finally have abolished capital punishment. By the same token, it is sad that there are strong political pressures to reinstate it. In such a context, it is even more astounding that Nagarjuna should have set forth this clear-cut principle almost two thousand years ago, in such specific, practical terms.

Nagarjuna has already given specific advice regarding socialistic universal welfare policy: "Cause the blind, the sick, the humble, the unprotected, the destitute, and the crippled, all equally to attain food and drink without omission." He does not elaborate upon this in specific policy terms. It is perfectly clear that he considers it obvious that the king is obligated to care for everyone in the whole nation as if they were his children. In modern terms, the welfare system created by Roosevelt in the United States, and the welfare socialism the socialist states have implemented, fit extremely well with this policy. But recently, we can observe a trend of assumption that, while any reasonable person would like to give everything to everyone, it is bad for people to get goods for nothing, and it is impossible to support everyone; there is not enough wealth for that purpose. The assumptions underlying this anti-welfare reaction we see around the world are that (1) people are inherently lazy, and (2) wealth is inherently insufficient. Indeed, there were certainly such attitudes in Nagarjuna's day and earlier. The central Buddhist story of Prince Vessantara turns on the paradox of generosity and wealth. Everyone loves him because he gives everyone everything they ask for. Yet the nation comes to fear him when it seems he will give away even the very sources of their wealth. So they shrink back in fright, clutch what they have to themselves, and banish their real source of joy, the generous Prince.

Since the welfare system was installed in the United States, that nation has produced the greatest wealth ever produced by any nation in history, including inventions in principle capable of infinite productivity; and this in the midst of a series of disastrous wars, with their aftermaths wherein the nation gave enormous treasure to rebuild the nations it had defeated. Now, the rulers of America confusedly think that their gifts to the people, the real source of their optimism, the energy of real productivity, are exhausting them, and so they want to take it all away. In this confused effort to clutch onto what they see as scarce and shrinking wealth, they will destroy the source of that wealth, the love and optimistic confidence and creativity of the people. Fortunately, this will result in a rapid disaster for all, so the error will soon come to light, and Prince Vessantara will return in triumph from his banishment. Hoarding creates poverty. Giving away creates wealth. Imagination of scarcity is thus the cause of loss. Imagination of abundance creates endless wealth. It is terrible or wonderful, depending on one's tolerance, that life must always be so subtle, so paradoxical, and complex.

Nagarjuna seems to be aware of the charge of "impractical idealism" that tends to be levelled against his *Counsels,* and so his verses closing this passage address the practicality question. "In order to maintain control, oversee your country through the eyes of agents; attentive and mindful, always act in accordance with the principles." An effective intelligence system seems to be necessary! The king must know what is happening throughout his realm to prevent abuses and forestall disasters. In modern terms, Nagarjuna allows for the vital role of "intelligence," the gathering of insightful information about the state of the people. The very mention of an "Intelligence Agency" is so sensitive nowadays, it is hard to remember that it is not the "intelligence" but the stupidity and violence in the paramilitary activities of the CIA, KGB, and their colleagues in other nations that have caused their aura of horror. Theoretically, if the responsible leaders of all nations really had all the information about all consequences of their actions, they surely would desist from the foolish and self-destructive policies they currently espouse.

Furthermore, another role of intelligence is to find out what people are doing in a positive direction, to reinforce their heroisms and virtuous accomplishments. "Always handsomely reward those firm in virtues with rich gifts, honors, and advancements, while treating all others in just proportion." A reward system providing positive reinforcement for virtue is an indispensable part of any system of law, as any parent knows. Modern systems of justice have become so obsessed with their catch-and-punish functions, they do not even consider this within their province. Presidents and generals award medals, the news media commend acts of heroism and even more humdrum virtue as "human interest," and there are economic rewards for some achievements and social rewards of peer esteem for virtue. But there is no merit system that responds to people's good actions comparable to the criminal system that responds to their mistakes. The last such systems are probably the knighthood system remaining in those few lands such as Britain where the traditional idea of hierarchical social solidarity has not totally disappeared. In democratic lands the only positive incentive is probably money. So perhaps Nagarjuna is merely suggesting that the Department of Justice include a branch that seeks out instances of virtue to be rewarded and not spend all its energy on cases of crimes for punishment!

Nagarjuna sums up his practical counsels with a pleasant metaphor: "The birds of the populace will alight upon the royal tree that gives the cool shade of tolerance, that flourishes with the flowers of honors, and that provides the bounteous fruit of great rewards." That is, an idealistic social policy is realistic. Tolerance, justice, and generosity are not merely lofty ideals, "ultra-obligations" for a few saints and heroes to aspire to embody, but are the essential components of any viable social policy. The ruler or government must manifest them first, and each citizen must strive to cultivate them. Since animals' habits do not automatically tend away from anger, delusion, and greed toward tolerance, justice, and giving, these virtues must gradually be cultivated. As each must do this for himself or herself, individualistic transcendentalism is the foundation of any viable activism. From this basis, pacifism is the social expression of tolerance; educational universalism is the social expression of wise justice; and socialistic sharing of wealth is the social expression of generosity.

These four principles seem to encompass mainstream Buddhist social practice, as counselled by Nagarjuna. These four guidelines should be reliable in choosing a line of action in particular situations. It is always essential to remember, however, the fundamental inconceivability of all things, for which great love seems finally the only adequate response. Nagarjuna insists that "the profound, enlightenment in practice, is emptiness creative as compassion." Jesus Christ's "Love God with all thy heart, and thy neighbor as thyself," and Augustine's "Love God and do what you will"—these two great "pivotal phrases" are very much in the same vein, using of course the theistic term for emptiness. In a culture more used to those great statements, we might express Nagarjuna as follows: "Open thy heart to absolute emptiness, and love all thy neighbors as thyself!" It is such love that is the whole "Law," and is the very body of all Buddhas. Vimalakirti describes it to Manjusri:

> The love that is firm, its high resolve unbreakable like a diamond;...the love that is never exhausted because it acknowledges voidness and selflessness; the love that is generosity because it bestows the gift of Truth without the tight fist of bad teachers; the love that is justice because it benefits immoral beings; the love that is tolerance because it protects both self and others; the love that is enterprise because it takes responsibility for all living things; the love that is meditation because it refrains from indulgence in tastes; the love that is wisdom because it causes attainment at the proper time; the love that is liberative technique because it shows the way everywhere; the love that is without formality because it is pure in motivation; the love that is without deviation because it acts decisively; the love that is high resolve because it is free of passions; the love that is without deceit because it is not artificial; the love that is happiness because it introduces living beings to the happiness of a Buddha. Such, Manjusri, is the great love of a bodhisattva.[12]

NOTES

[1]All Nagarjuna references are from Nagarjuna, *The Precious Garland*, translated by Jeffrey Hopkins (London: Allen & Unwin, 1975). I have, however, used the Sanskrit original (Vaidya, 1960) in certain places, and on that basis altered the terminology to suit my own preference, thus to maintain coherence between quotes and commentary. [*Ed. note*: For the verse number of each quote from Nagarjuna, see Professor Thurman's article from which this essay is excerpted, published in *The Eastern Buddhist*, Vol. XVI, No. 1, Spring 1983.]

[2]I use "Universal" and "Individual" to translate *Maha-* and *Hina-* , based on the fact that the Mahayana is a vehicle designed for riders who wish all other beings to share the ride, and the hinayana is a vehicle designed for riders who also hope others will get aboard, but who are primarily concerned with hanging on themselves at least. The former thus emphasizes "Universal" liberation, the latter "Individual" liberation. Finally, since universal liberation certainly cannot take place unless it is "universal individual" liberations in totality, these translations also capture the relationship between the two vehicles.

[3]Sanskrit *pudgala-* and *dharma-nairatmya* are usually translated "personal selflessness" and "phenomenal selflessness." However, *dharma* includes *noumena*, i.e. non-apparent, even non-visualizable, mental objects, such as "emptiness," "absolute," "infinite," "eternity," and so forth, which are still selfless. Therefore, I am inclining toward the translations "subjective" and "objective" selflessness.

[4]The close correspondence between the tenfold path of evolutionary action and the Mosaic Decalogue is striking and should be more thoroughly studied.

[5]Four famous works by Nagarjuna in Sanskrit.

[6]See note 2 above. It is worth emphasis that the Individual Vehicle monastic institution is itself the most "socially activist" institution in history, designed and normally functioning as a direct antidote to militarism in numerous civilizations. Contrary to the view that considers the Universal Vehicle as opposed to the Individual Vehicle, the former requires

the latter as essential in achieving its goal of world-transformation. Thus, Vimalakirti, while providing individual monks with critiques of their various one-sided views, respects each of them as monks, members of the Community, never losing sight of the sanctity of the monastic institution.

[7]It is often hard to find a single source that communicates the ambience of the Satavahana civilization. One has to study the scupture of Amaravata and tha Ajanta paintings, then use the imagination. The southern world of the *Gandavyuha* can be evoked from the text, then one can take a literary cross-fix from the *Katha* narratives, Tamil poetry, and the Chinese pilgrim's accounts. The overall *rasa*, or aesthetic taste, that emerges from these imaginative exercises is one of a lush gentleness, in stark contrast with the more militaristic north Indian lands.

[8]R. B. Fuller is fond of making this point in his essays in *Utopia or Oblivion*.

[9]Verses 301-345.

[10]Vasubandhu gives this illuminating analysis of the Sanskrit *dharma* in his little-known work, the *Vyakhyayukti*, a treatise on the hermeneutics of sutra interpretation, preserved in the Tibetan *bsTan 'Gyur*.

[11]When speaking of Buddha in the context of ideal archetypes, it is important to use the double pronoun, as a modern Buddhist, for males not to monopolize access to religious virtuosity and spiritual perfection. In fact, the 112 super-human signs of a Buddha contain definite symbols of androgyny, subliminally resonating with the famous pronouncement that "ultimate reality is beyond male and female," found in many Universal Vehicle Scriptures.

[12]Thurman, *The Holy Teaching of Vimalakirti* (University Park: Penn State, 1976) p. 57.

ROBERT AITKEN

Three Lessons From Shaku Soen

Shaku Soen Zenji, abbot of Enkaku Zen Monastery in Kamakura, Japan, addressed the World's Parliament of Religions at the Columbian Exposition in Chicago in 1893 on the subject, "Arbitration Instead of War," declaring:

> We are not born to fight one against another. We are born to enlighten our wisdom and cultivate our virtues according to the guidance of truth. And happily we see the movement toward the abolition of war and the establishment of a peace-making society. But how will truth be realized? Simply by the help of the religion of truth. The religion of truth is the fountain of benevolence and mercy....We must not make any distinction between race and race, between civilization and civilization, between creed and creed, and faith and faith....All beings in the universe are in the bosom of truth. We are all sisters and brothers; we are sons and daughters of truth, and let us understand one another and be true sons and daughters of truth. Truth be praised."[1]

However, 11 years later, when Japan declared war against Russia, Shaku Soen wrote:

> War is an evil, and a great one indeed. But war against evils must be unflinchingly prosecuted until we reach the final aim. In the present

hostilities, into which Japan has entered with great reluctance, she seeks no egoistic purpose, but seeks the subjugation of evils hostile to civilization, peace, and enlightenment."[2]

Thus Shaku Soen could distinguish between civilization and civilization and subordinate his concern for peace to the economic and political compulsions of his nation-state. He accompanied troops to Manchuria, saying:

> I came here with a double purpose. I wished to have my faith tested by going through the greatest horrors of life, but I also wished to inspire, if I could, our valiant soldiers with the ennobling thoughts of the Buddha, so as to enable them to die on the battlefield with the confidence that the task in which they are engaged is great and noble.[3]

These quotations must be set in context in order to understand their contradiction. The World's Parliament of Religions was the first and greatest in scope of all ecumenical gatherings. Its message was understanding and peace among people, whatever their differences, and Shaku Soen, finding within his own tradition strong support for the purposes of the Parliament, felt free to express this support quite specifically. A decade later, however, the political climate of Japan was fervent, if not jingoistic, and he obviously considered it his duty as a religious leader to encourage those at the forefront of the conflict to give themselves to the fight wholeheartedly so that, even in dying, they would be free of doubt and internal conflict.

Examining Shaku Soen's religious tradition, we find that from the very beginning, the function of Japanese Buddhism was to support the nation-state and its institutions. The Seventeen Article Constitution of Shotoku Taishi, promulgated in 604 C.E., insists upon reverence to the Three Treasures of Buddhism and on the practice of Confucian hierarchy of lord over vassal, with the emperor over all: "When you receive the imperial commands, fail not to carry them out scrupulously. Let there be a want of care in this matter, and ruin is the natural consequence."[4]

Theodore de Bary, in his *Buddhist Tradition*, stresses that the counterstream of *prajña* and peace was also present in early Japanese Buddhism in the form of the *Sutra of the Golden Light*, which "played a more important role than any other in establishing Buddhism as the religion of Japan," with an influence "undiminished for centuries":

> Know ye, Deva Kings, that the 84,000 rulers of the 84,000 cities, towns, and villages of the world shall each enjoy happiness of every sort in his own land; that they shall all possess freedom of action, and obtain all manner of precious things in abundance; that they shall never again invade each other's territories; that they shall receive recompense in accordance with their deeds of previous existences; that they shall no longer yield to the evil desire of taking the land of others; that they shall learn that the smaller their desires, the greater the blessing; that they shall emancipate themselves from the suffering of warfare and bondage...
>
> In this way, the nations of the world shall live in peace and prosperity; the peoples shall flourish, the earth shall be made fertile, the climate temperate, and the seasons shall follow in the proper order.[5]

The Sutra of the Golden Light is clearly a precedent for Shaku Soen's words before the World's Parliament of Religions, while Shotoku Taishi's Constitution provides the base for his support of Emperor Meiji's declaration of war against Russia. But why did he revert to the latter, lesser source in 1904?

I think the answer lies partly in the status of Buddhism as a foreign guest in Japan. Tokugawa Ieyasu (1542-1616), founder of the Tokugawa shogunate, is said to have written: "My body and the body of others were born in the Empire of the Gods. Therefore, to accept the teaching of other countries, such as Confucian, Buddhist, or Taoist doctrines—and to apply one's whole and undivided attention to them, would be in short to desert one's own master and transfer one's loyalty to another. Is not this to forget the origin of one's being?"[6]

Charles Eliot comments on this passage, "Ieyasu's statement should be intelligible to a Western statesman."[7] And indeed, East or West, nation-states have assumed bottom-line authority over organized religions, banning Buddhism altogether for periods in China, breaking up the Jodo-Shin sect when it grew large, and confiscating monastery lands in Japan, suppressing Catholicism in England, forbidding polygamy among Mormons in the United States. Examples appear in every century, East and West.

What do we learn from all this, as American Buddhists? I see three lessons. First, it seems generally true that Expatriate Buddhism, the religion of immigrant Japanese and their descendents, has followed the ancient standards of loyalty to government and its institutions which Ieyasu set down; it has transferred rather unquestioning allegiance from Japanese emperor to American president. Expatriate Buddhism is mainstream American in cultural outlook, and such fundamental conservatism actually challenges the Way of the Buddha. Treating our Bodhisattva vows seriously, we must respond to America's stockpiling of nuclear weapons, its materialism, its profligate consumption of energy, its destruction of forests and animals, and its depersonalization of life.

Second, Buddhists of Western birth too are "guests" in the United States. Even those of us born and raised in WASP households are somehow socially "beyond the pale," often vaguely suspect, sometimes tarred with the same brush as Scientology, the Children of God, the Unification Church, and Ananda Marga. Buddhists in Japan responded to the danger of bad public relations by setting to one side the full implications of their vows, either isolating themselves behind monastery walls or joining wholeheartedly in the compulsions of the larger society. We can learn from this negative example to maintain our integrity as Buddhists, seeking good public relations as far as integrity permits but standing fast and saying NO! to our country's rush toward nuclear war and biological holocaust.

Third, whether we are socially secure or not, we must make sure that the *prajña* and peace of our great tradition and of our minds are not overcome by the demands of society. In studying the sociology of Buddhism in China and Japan, it is clear that the vow to save all beings was sometimes construed as an existential expression somehow limited by the monastery walls or even to private devotions. Surely the time has come for us to acknowledge that the unity and love we experience in our practice extends to all people and all creatures of this earth. The *Sutra of the Golden Light* may be our guide in understanding that you and I are ultimately the "rulers" who practice harmony and enjoy peace with all beings, as we turn the Wheel of the Dharma in the *dojo*, in the marketplace, and in political forums.

NOTES

[1]Shaku Soen. "Arbitration Instead of War." *The World's Parliament of Religions*; ed. John Henry Barrows. (Chicago: The Parliament Publishing Co., 1893), p. 1285.

[2]Shaku Soen. *Sermons of a Buddhist Abbot*; trans. D. T. Suzuki. (New York: Samuel Weiser, Inc., 1971), p. 201.

[3]*Ibid.*, p. 203.

[4]Theodore de Bary, ed. *The Buddhist Tradition: In India, China, and Japan.* (New York: The Modern Library, 1969), p. 260.

[5]*Ibid.*, p. 271.

[6]Adapted from Charles Eliot. *Japanese Buddhism.* (London: Routledge, Kegan Paul, 1935), p. 193.

[7]*Ibid.*, p. 194.

FRED EPPSTEINER

In the Crucible:
The Precepts of the Order of Interbeing

The First Precept. Do not be idolatrous about or bound to any doctrine, theory, or ideology, even Buddhist ones. Buddhist systems of thought are guiding means; they are not absolute truth.

The Second Precept. Do not think the knowledge you presently possess is changeless, absolute truth. Avoid being narrow-minded and bound to present views. Learn and practice non-attachment from views in order to be open to receive others' viewpoints. Truth is found in life and not merely in conceptual knowledge. Be ready to learn throughout your entire life and to observe reality in yourself and in the world at all times.

The Third Precept. Do not force others, including children, by any means whatsoever, to adopt your views, whether by authority, threat, money, propaganda or even education. However, through compassionate dialogue, help others renounce fanaticism and narrowness.

The Fourth Precept. Do not avoid contact with suffering or close your eyes before suffering. Do not lose awareness of the existence of suffering in the life of the world. Find ways to be with those who are suffering by all means, including personal contact and visits, images, sound. By such means, awaken yourself and others to the reality of suffering in the world.

The Fifth Precept. Do not accumulate wealth while millions are hungry. Do not take as the aim of your life fame, profit, wealth or sensual pleasure. Live simply and share time, energy and material resources with those who are in need.

The Sixth Precept. Do not maintain anger or hatred. As soon as anger and hatred arise, practice the meditation on compassion in order to deeply understand the persons who have caused anger and hatred. Learn to look at other beings with the eyes of compassion.

The Seventh Precept. Do not lose yourself in dispersion and in your surroundings. Learn to practice breathing in order to regain composure of body and mind, to practice mindfulness and to develop concentration and understanding.

The Eighth Precept. Do not utter words that can create discord and cause the community to break. Make every effort to reconcile and resolve all conflicts, however small.

The Ninth Precept. Do not say untruthful things for the sake of personal interest or to impress people. Do not utter words that cause division and hatred. Do not spread news that you do not know to be certain. Do not criticize or condemn things that you are not sure of. Always speak truthfully and constructively. Have the courage to speak out about situations of injustice, even when doing so may threaten your own safety.

The Tenth Precept. Do not use the Buddhist community for personal gain or profit, or transform your community into a political party. A religious community, however, should take a clear stand against oppression and injustice and should strive to change the situation without engaging in partisan conflicts.

The Eleventh Precept. Do not live with a vocation that is harmful to humans and nature. Do not invest in companies that deprive others of their chance to live. Select a vocation which helps realize your ideal of compassion.

The Twelfth Precept. Do not kill. Do not let others kill. Find whatever means possible to protect life and to prevent war.

The Thirteenth Precept. Possess nothing that should belong to others. Respect the property of others, but prevent others from enriching themselves from human suffering or the suffering of other beings.

The Fourteenth Precept. Do not mistreat your body. Learn to handle it with respect. Do not look on your body as only an instrument. Preserve vital energies (sexual, breath, spirit) for the realization of the Way. Sexual expression should not happen without love and commitment. In sexual relationships, be aware of future suffering that may be caused. To preserve the happiness of others, respect the rights and commitments of others. Be fully aware of the responsibility of bringing new lives into the world. Meditate on the world into which you are bringing new beings.

The fourteen precepts of the Order of Interbeing are a unique expression of traditional Buddhist morality coming to terms with contemporary issues. They were not developed by secluded monks attempting to update the traditional Buddhist precepts. Rather, they were forged in the crucible of war and devastation that was the daily experience for many Southeast Asians during the past several decades.

In 1964, responding to burgeoning hatred, intolerance, and suffering, a group of Vietnamese Buddhists, many deeply grounded in Buddhist philosophy and meditation, founded an Order to become an instrument of their vision of engaged Buddhism. Composed of monks and nuns, laymen and laywomen, the Order of Interbeing never comprised great numbers, yet its influence and effects were deeply felt within their country. Highly motivated and deeply committed, members of the Order and their supporters organized anti-war demonstrations, printed leaflets and books, ran social service projects, organized an underground for draft resisters, and cared for many of the war's suffering, innocent victims.

During the war, many members and supporters died, some from self-immolation, some from cold-blooded murder, and some from the indiscriminate murder of war. At this time, it is impossible to say whether any remnant of the Order still exists in Asia, even though several members did emigrate to the West, and have recently ordained a number of Westerners and Vietnamese refugees. Yet these Fourteen Precepts that they recited weekly, while war, political repression, and immense suffering tore apart their familiar world, are now being offered to us.

Existing at a time when their people and country were being destroyed in the name of supposedly irreconcilable "isms," the Order was acutely aware of the need for all people to realize the commonality of their experience and to renounce all views that posited One Truth or One Way. Therefore, the first three precepts of their Order directly reject fanaticism and political or religious self-righteousness. Even Buddhism, they say, is not the Truth, but solely a means to the realization of it.

The fourth precept goes to the heart of Buddhist compassion and directs a challenge to all practitioners. Is it enough to practice formal Dharma in order that some day in the future we will be able to help all living beings? Or, rather, can the suffering of these beings diminish through our compassionate involvement in the present? This precept seems to imply that contemplative reflections on the suffering of living beings is not enough, and that the lotus can grow only when planted deep in the mud. I remember once talking to a Vietnamese monk about Kuan-Yin, the Bodhisattva of Compassion. He remarked that people mistakenly think that the only way to worship her is by putting offerings in front of her image and praying. Holding up his own hands and looking directly in my eyes, he said, "These are the best offerings one can give Kuan-Yin."

The fifth precept suggests that Right Livelihood has implications beyond simply avoiding the forbidden professions, and that the manner in which we spend our time, energy, and resources is as much a moral problem as a practical one. The sixth precept is similar to the traditional Buddhist precept concerning anger, except that it challenges us directly to apply an antidote as soon as anger arises. This impresses us with the far-reaching social effects of individual anger. The seventh precept addresses the question of how Buddhist activists can maintain their practice in the midst of activity. The answer is traditional—practice mindfulness, awareness, and regulating the breath. This implies that the inner practice of the social activist is no different from that of the hermit. Only their external conditions can be contrasted.

Speaking directly to the Southeast Asian situation are the eighth and ninth precepts. Brothers fighting brothers; communities rent by political, social, and religious division; factions within the Sangha; spies everywhere. These two precepts provide a model for Right Speech and Right Activity, while never losing track of the need to speak out about social injustice and oppression for the all-embracing, non-partisan viewpoint of Dharma, in interdependence of all life.

The twelfth precept, a reformulation of the traditional Buddhist precept against killing, states that not only are we enjoined not to kill life, but we are equally obligated to protect it. And does not the thirteenth precept on non-stealing imply that the well-stocked shelves of one country relate directly to the empty shelves of another? Or that profit-making at the cost of human suffering and the suffering of other beings is an immoral activity? Interestingly, the final precept deals with sexuality, especially since many of the Order's members were monks and nuns. This precept seems to imply that respecting life and committing oneself to ending suffering is as real an issue within the most intimate of human relationships as in the political and social arenas.

In summary, it could be said that these fourteen precepts issue a clarion call of Emptiness and Non-ego in action. Each precept is permeated with the understanding that concepts, thoughts, and actions are inherently impermanent and insubstantial. Each precept enjoins a form of moral action that is based on non-separation and an unceasingly aware state of compassion. Not holding onto a notion of self, we are invited to engage ourselves courageously in the world, to see the nature of suffering clearly, and with discriminating awareness to undertake the task of liberating all beings.

CAO NGOC PHUONG

Days and Months

August 4, 1971

Dear Sister Mai,

I still remember the July afternoon five years ago when I stopped by to see you on my way home from picking up the pledge money for the School of Youth for Social Service. When you spoke, Chi Mai, your voice was filled with affection and your unique blend of wisdom and innocence that we began to call "the special voice of Chi Mai." "Phuong! Where have you been? You're totally covered with sweat."

You knit your eyebrows and pouted your lips like an adult pampering a young child. I laughed, "What do you mean? I've only been to Tan Dinh Market to pick up the monthly pledges for the School. You make it sound like I have been working in the rice fields!" You laughed and gestured for me to come inside and sit down, and you brought me a glass of ice water—exactly what I was wishing for.

On that day you wore a robe like the nuns in the pagoda, and you looked so beautiful. After a little small talk, I asked you what you thought about the appeal Thây Nhat Hanh[1] had just launched in Washington, D.C. asking both North and South

Vietnam to declare a ceasefire and demanding that the Americans withdraw all their troops. You sat silently for a moment and then, while smoothing my hair back, said, "Phuong, dear, I love and respect Thây. I feel very close to his ideas about social service and that is why I follow him. But his political activities worry me."

I understood, Chi Mai. Thây's appeal for peace was still very "early." A "patriot" wouldn't dare demand the Americans withdraw their soldiers, and the government and newspapers strongly attacked Thây's statement. You were the youngest child in a well-to-do family and were very close with your parents. You'd never had the chance to visit the villages in the midst of the war. How could you not feel worried when the Saigon radio, daily newspapers, and even the President himself, accused Thây of being a Communist, even though you respected Thây so much?

On the point of tears, I trembled as I spoke, "Consider this, Chi Mai. Buddha teaches us to love all beings, even animals. We're not supposed to harm even a fly. But people are killing each other. How can we just sit by? Vietnam is 4,000 years old. When did we ever need the Americans to repel invaders? We managed to chase the Chinese away ourselves, so effectively they almost seemed to fly. Chi Mai, do you know that when the Prayer for Peace was carried in the *Buddhist Weekly* in 1964, eight young people went to the Central Executive Committee of the Unified Buddhist Church and offered to fast to the death in order to pray for peace if the Church would agree to our action? I was one of those eight who vowed to fast, Chi Mai. But Thich Tam Chau yelled at us very loudly, and the Council did not give their consent, so we didn't dare do it. We were afraid that, without the Church's backing, our action would be fruitless."

You interrupted: "Of course they didn't! How could the monks agree to such a thing? You've still got an aged mother to care for." But I argued with you, "I know that I would incur the sin of impiety towards my mother if I brought death upon myself, but if our deaths might shorten the war by a few years and save countless other lives, I will pay for the sin of impiety in another life."

I always spoke well enough, but sometimes I could not yet act as I spoke! After my words, you sat silently for a long time. You bent your face downwards; and then, after a long moment, you raised it and held my two hands firmly in yours. "Phuong, you're right! You have spoken most truly." You looked at me and paused before speaking again, "I want to make the same vow. The Church has forbidden the first vow, but if there is ever another time, you can count me in."

Your words moved me so, and I wept. You were not part of the "wave of new Buddhists" like the rest of us. You had not struggled with the same problems that we younger ones had in coming to Buddhism. But you had a special quality—you were not afraid to frankly criticize whomever you disagreed with. You always listened intently, and if what was said seemed right, you went ahead and acted, while the rest of us continued to debate.

A few months after that, you became involved in the student peace movement at Van Hanh University. Even before that, you helped to distribute copies of *Lotus in a Sea of Fire*, which had encouraged and inspired you in your efforts for peace. You hid it in your white Volkswagen to circulate 10 copies to this school, 20 to that one, and little by little the book made its way into the hands of every teacher and student organization you knew. I was very moved by your taking on such a task, because as the daughter of an upper class family, you had never worked clandestinely like that before.

One day in late 1966, I don't remember exactly which month, you invited me to your room after we had recited sutras at the pagoda. You took my hand and said, "I've got an idea, and I want to know what you think about it. There were eight friends, including yourself, who were willing to fast to the death for peace in 1964. I make nine and if I can find another person we'll be ten. Ten of us can each go to a different city and, on the same day, disembowel ourselves as a sacrifice for peace. We can leave behind an appeal for peace which will shake ten prominent spots in our country and move the hearts of people everywhere. Fasting and immolation no longer shock people."

I promised you that I would tell the others about your proposal and think it over myself, but inside I already knew there would be difficulties in realizing it. Last time, all of us were single. Now several had husbands or wives and others lived far away. I suspected there would only be you and me.

I stayed in my room for four days to reflect. Finally I reasoned with you on every consideration possible as to why we shouldn't do it: The peace movement was still weak. If we sacrificed ourselves the only thing we could be sure of was that our brothers and sisters in the peace movement would be minus you and me. In addition to our peace work, there was our responsibility to Thây Thanh Van. Thây Nhat Hanh had entrusted him with running the School of Youth for Social Service, and we had promised to help him, at least until the first students completed their training. Even though Thây Nhat Hanh was no longer working at the school, his appeal for peace had caused the School a lot of difficulty. It was so poor. Several hundred students were trying to survive on just white rice and soy sauce, and often there was not even enough of that to go around. Chi Mai, you and I had promised to find rice for the School. Our absence would be a deadly blow to Thây Thanh Van and to all of our friends. In 1964, I was willing to sacrifice myself because the Buddhist movement was becoming strong and, with the backing of the Church, we had hopes of realizing our desire. I didn't have any worries about the School then, either.

I spoke just as sincerely, with all my heart, for our lives, as I had for my sacrifice then, and you were moved to abandon the idea, but wanted a final word from Thây Nhat Hanh. (You told me that you had sent a letter asking his permission and hadn't received an answer yet.) You said, "Well, I guess we'll need to work a lot harder, right Phuong? You must make me work more. You are so good at doing things. You can do anything. It upsets me that I can't work as you do!"

Your last sentence irritated me. "Work like me? Oh, Chi Mai! I can't work like you, so how can you work like me? We each have our own way. If you don't stop talking like that, I will just give up!" You laughed so gently and took my hand, "Oh, Phuong, really!" A week later, you told me that Thây Nhat Hanh had written, also forbidding the sacrifice.

On the first day of the second year of the School, we teachers and the students gathered at the newly built campus in Phu Tho Hoa. We numbered nearly 300 but there was no more than 1,000 piasters in our treasury—not enough to buy even one sack of rice. On Saturday night, the Sisters and Brothers in the Order of Interbeing gathered privately, after meditating together, to discuss the School's finances. Thây Thanh Van did not want the students to know or worry about our financial crisis. He wanted to shoulder the entire responsibility himself. Hearing the voices of students out on the veranda, we felt all the more worry and affection for them.

One day Mai Sa and Tai came to recite the precepts with us. It was your turn to lead the ceremony. When you reached the twelfth precept: "Do not kill. Do not let others kill. Find whatever means possible to protect life....," your voice faltered. From that point to the end of the reading, you spoke so softly it was nearly impossible to hear you. Your concentration seemed to disappear. Can it be that at that very moment you decided to sacrifice yourself for peace, Chi Mai?

Afterwards, as we were putting the precept books back on the shelves, Chi Uyen asked you, "Did something happen to you today, Chi Mai?" And I added, "You seemed to lose your concentration while reading. Are you all right?" You just smiled and asked if you could return to your room early.

The following two Saturdays you did not come to our weekly day of mindfulness. Chi Uyen's mother and my own mother didn't want us to come to the pagoda, either. They were afraid strangers might come and murder us, as they had other friends. But we were determined to make our families understand the importance of coming to the pagoda. I assumed that your parents were reluctant to let you come and spend the night with us, especially since you were the youngest and most beloved child in your family. When you didn't show up the third Saturday, I thought that even if your parents did not want you to spend the night, you could at least recite the precepts with us during the afternoon.

I wondered if something was wrong. I was a little angry with you for not taking the days of mindfulness more seriously. You could at least have told us if you were too busy to come. No one had seen you for three weeks! You didn't even attend the School staff meeting. You seemed even to forget your peace work with the other students in the Faculty of Science and Letters.

Then on Sunday morning, May 14, 1967, you came. I was still in my room, reading, with the window opened onto the field of grass and green bamboo. Because my door was shut, I didn't hear your car pull up. Chi Uyen came into my room and quietly said, "Phuong, Chi Mai is here and she's wearing a beautiful violet dress with gold embroidery!" I closed my book. I wanted to come out and scold you. Just the day before, I promised the others that I would stop by your house to see if you were ill. There couldn't be any other reason for you abandoning us for so long. As I walked out of my room, you were surrounded by friends. Everyone had something they wanted to tell you, and people were following you into your room.

When I joined them, you were cutting and passing around a banana cake. Your hair was arranged in a beautiful bun and you were wearing a brand-new violet *ao dai* with gold embroidery. You looked as if you were about to attend an important ceremony. I asked, "You brought the banana cake, Chi Mai?" Then I laughed and said, teasingly, "What could have caused you to abandon us for three weeks, not even coming to our days of mindfulness, and now you are dressed so beautifully, bringing a delicious cake to treat us? Are you getting ready to leave us and get married?" Others chimed in, "Very possible! Chi Mai looks so pretty today!" We all laughed, but you just smiled and didn't say a word. Then you left. I felt sad and ashamed, and resolved to come to the pagoda on Tuesday morning, at least for a short time, in order to make you happy. But I was still annoyed when I thought of your violet dress with the golden embroidery, your not coming to the mindfulness days for three weeks, and your not returning to the School and seeing any of your friends.

It was not until Ngoc brought your final letters and poems to me that I was able to understand why we had not seen you for three weeks. I realized that you had wanted to spend that time with your mother and father in order to give them the sweetest, most precious moments and hours a loving child can offer. For three weeks you were, as our folk poetry sings, sweet bananas, fragrant rice, and precious honey for your parents. And during those three weeks you prepared for your sacrifice alone.

Ngoc ran frantically that morning to my house to tell me you had immolated yourself. I was so shocked I could not say a word. Only after a long silence could I speak, and in a calm voice, I said, "She has sacrificed herself for Peace."

My mother sat beside me, silently. After a few minutes she burst into tears and cried, "My God, how can she have done that to her parents? Her parents are still alive, and her act will lead them both to the grave!" She looked at me as she wept. I knew she was not really condemning you, Chi Mai. She was crying for the days when her own "activist" daughter might follow in your steps. Without saying anything, I put on a dress and went out; for there was much that needed to be done. In the evening, when I returned, I told my mother of the time you had suggested we dis-embowel ourselves and how I had argued against it. After that my mother calmed down, and she told me I must find ways with all my being to realize your prayer for Peace.

First I went to see your parents. Huynh Tinh Cu'a Street seemed as if it had been turned upside down. When I entered your house, your parents embraced me and wept. I don't know who brought them the news. Your mother fainted several times, but she still made a great effort to go with your father and me in the car to the pagoda. When we arrived, your parents went into the pagoda, but I ran down to the Cau Muoi Market. I don't know why, but I did not dare to enter the pagoda and see you in death. I just wanted to immerse myself in work. I went to tell all of our friends of your sacrifice. There were many aunts and uncles in the markets, all poor workers, who loved us dearly. When I found Aunt Ba, I took her hand and said: "My Sister Mai has immolated herself. She's already dead, Aunt Ba."

Only at that moment was I finally able to weep, and Aunt Ba wept with me. You remember Co Ba? She sold areca nuts in a tiny dark corner of the market. When she heard the news of your death, she cried out, "No, you cannot mean our own Mai, my child? God!" Soon everyone in the market was disturbed, and crying. Although Co Ba had just a tiny space in the market, everyone respected her great virtue and merit. She kept tiger balm and a spoon ready at all times in case someone fell ill and needed their back to be rubbed. People came to her at any hour of the night, and she never refused to take care of them. Because of that, whenever she gave a "command," the others in the market gave their full support at once. I don't know how many tons of vegetables she was able to gather for the pagodas and the School of Youth for Social Service just by asking all the vendors to donate left-over vegetables. If you wanted anything, all you needed to do was ask Co Ba, and the whole market would be at your service. She said to me, "You go on, my child. I'll follow at once."

Co Ba walked with me to the front of the market and waved her hand to several pedicab and Lambretta drivers. She spoke only a few words to each of them and they turned on their motors and prepared to carry people from the market to the Tu' Nghiem Pagoda to visit you for the last time. In the first shuttle, there were five taxis and seven pedicabs. Everyone wept along the way, Chi Mai. "Miss Mai was so kind, so good! How can we bear this?" "Why do they go on fighting each other all the time, so that now Miss Mai has immolated herself to ask for Peace?" "Why does a person from a fine, educated family sacrifice herself for Peace, while we small fish of the sea are afraid to die, afraid to get arrested, and never dare to make sacrifices?"

Uncle Thieu Son came to the pagoda as well, with several other friends who were poor laborers, to pay their last respects to you. Uncle's face was worn and tired. When he saw me, he could only say, "Niece!" and tears rolled gently down his cheeks. The manager of the printing shop who had refused to help us print peace documents was also there. She came up to me weeping and said that she would help us in any way we needed. Even important officials in the government came and offered to find ways to help our work for peace. Only then I realized my eloquent argument against sacrificing ourselves, before ("We are too few. If we are gone, there will not be enough of us to do the work.") was utterly wrong. Your single sacrifice moved the hearts of countless others, Chi Mai, and made the peace movement swell like waves in a storm. Even friends who had joined the jungle guerrillas and had disappeared for a long time, sent back news and asked, "How can we help realize Mai's wish and bring reconciliation?"

In front of you, you placed two statues, the Virgin Mary and the Bodhisattva Quan The Am . In your poems and letters, you asked Catholics and Buddhists to work together for Peace so that people might inherit the love of Jesus and the compassion of Buddha.

I think about Thây Tri Quang. It was 11 years from the time I first knew Thây until the day you sacrificed yourself, but I never had seen him more moved. At 1:00 in the morning he sent a message to Tu Nghiem Pagoda to ask the nuns to provide a car for me to come to An Quang Pagoda. (Thây was afraid I would be arrested or kidnapped otherwise.) There was no driver for the car, so Tai had to walk me there. When we got there, the Pagoda gate was locked, and we had to climb over it to get in. When I got to Thây's room, he was playing with a tape recorder. He said, "Although this machine doesn't record very clearly, I want to have a tape of someone reading all the poems and letters of the person who has sacrificed herself so that I may know her better. Can you help me by reading them? I want the person who reads them to have a voice close to Mai's—a young girl's voice from the South."

The next day, at 4:00 in the morning, Thây disguised himself in a novice's robe and had someone take him to Tu Nghiem Pagoda. (Thây had been under house arrest for a long time. We were afraid he would be kidnapped or assassinated.) There he chanted sutras for you before your coffin. When he finished, he called me into the pagoda and said, "You must find every way to print Mai's letters and distribute them widely. I will pay for the paper and ink and printing costs. I don't have any money right now, but you can ask some of the Buddhist elders to lend you a little for me. I have a younger brother who teaches school. Each month for four months, he can give me 5,000 piasters to pay them back. Please try your best."

The following day Thây called me again, "Mai's prayer was for all religions to work together for peace. I've heard that Father Nguyen Ngoc Lan is a progressive Catholic and close to us. Can you ask him to write a preface to Mai's letters?" I was very moved; for in the past Thây had been quite skeptical about working with Catholics. In fact, without knowing Thây's thoughts, Father Lan had already come to see me and had offered to print your letters and write a foreword to them. He even accepted responsibility for circulating them, although that was a dangerous thing to do. Each time there was a heartfelt act like that, I thought of your round smiling face and I could hear you saying, "Isn't that wonderful, Phuong?" Just as you prayed for, the Venerables who led the Buddhist Church tried more every day to find opportunity to work with the Catholics, and the Catholics also began to have more sympathy and understanding for the Buddhists. And it all began with everyone's sympathy and understanding for you, Nhat Chi Mai.

It was fortunate that Ngoc brought me the copies of your letters that you had left for me, or else the only people who would have seen them would have been the police. Anh Khôn told us how that morning he came to the pagoda just as you had requested, to discover that you had just immolated yourself. The nuns were weeping and chanting sutras at the same time around you. And all Anh Khôn could do was stand without moving, as if he had been planted there. He wept without making a sound. He opened his mouth to speak, but no words came out, and he forgot even to take photos as you had requested him to do of the "ceremony." At that moment Anh Phuc and Anh Quan, the other two you had invited to the pagoda, arrived, but our three Brothers could only stand as though dead around you. They didn't notice that the police had arrived and were talking to the head nun. You were one of her dearest disciples and so when she heard that you had immolated yourself and the other nuns brought her copies of your letter addressed to eight friends, she fainted. (The notebook of letters with my name had already been taken by Ngoc.) The police confiscated all of your papers, but, luckily, they didn't know that you had also sent two tapes to Sister Giac Nhan addressed to your family and friends. (Sister Giac Nhan thought you were sending tapes of Buddhist music.)

The police also ordered that your body be taken to police headquarters, but Brothers Khon, Phuc, and Quan and others surrounded your body and prevented them from taking you away. The struggle went on for quite a while, and when the police could not carry out their orders, the head officer came and demanded your body. He was about to use force, when your parents arrived, just in time. Your father spoke strongly to him and asked him, "Please, in the name of her father, leave her in peace."

Throughout the three days you lay in Tu Nghiem, I tried to find ways to keep busy in order to avoid sitting beside you. I went to meet students both inside and outside our movement. I went to all the markets. I visited many organizations and friends. When I saw Sister T. H. Hiep and many other friends sitting, clutching the piece of the gold cloth which covered your body, and weeping, I still didn't have the courage to come near. I thought how my body should be lying next to yours or else in a pagoda in Hue, or Ben Tre, or Can Tho'. Hadn't that been your wish long ago? But here I was—I could still eat, drink, and sleep. How could I stand it?

All day long I met with groups and friends to inform them of your act. Each night, Mai Sa and I stayed up late translating your poems into English for newspapers and peace groups throughout the world. Students came in large numbers to the pagoda at night in order to take turns chanting sutras and watching your body, and to prevent the attempts of the police to confiscate your body. The moment a stranger entered the pagoda, one of the students made sure it was not someone coming to try to take you away. When the plot to confiscate your body did not work, the police tried to persuade your parents to bury you right way. They were afraid that if too much time lapsed, the news would travel to other provinces and there would be "difficulties." Your parents were certainly not worried about their threats. But your mother suffered greatly in her grief. Every day she fainted three or four times, and so your father and older brother wanted to bring you to An Duong Dia for the cremation earlier.

The day after your sacrifice, all the newspapers carried blank pages where the news of your act had been censored. The news of your sacrifice traveled solely by the mouths of Buddhists and friends. But even so, on the day of the cremation, many people came to the ceremony. The funeral car reached Phu Lam Bridge, but the line of people behind it stretched all the way back to Tu' Nghiem, a distance of five kilometers. Every student group and faculty, groups of small merchants and vendors from the markets, and old and experienced politicians were present. I was completely surprised to see many wealthy persons who before had accused us of being "Communists" or "Communist-controlled," now walking to accompany you to Phu Lam with tears in their eyes. There was a fine, cool rain. The white dresses of girl students, the black shirts of poor workers, the monks' and nuns' robes, the simple rags of our friends from the markets, and the fine clothes of the wealthy were all soaked by the gentle rain.

Thanh really has a gift to lighten even the saddest moments. She whispered in my ear: "Phuong, Phuong do you see Chi Mai? I can see her sitting on the funeral car looking down at the streams of friends, poor and rich, old and young. And seeing so many people, her face is bright and she is laughing, "Oh, Thanh this is so much fun! There are really a lot of people, aren't there? Isn't this a joyful occasion?" I had been walking in the rain like a robot, not thinking a thing. But when I heard Thanh's words, I felt pleased; for I knew it was exactly the kind of thing you would say.

I remember the poem you read over and over in the days before you immolated yourself—*Recommendation*, by Thây Nhat Hanh:

Promise me,
promise me this day
while the sun is just overhead
even as they strike you down
with a mountain of hate and
violence remember, brother
man is not our enemy.

Just your pity,
just your hate
invincible, limitless,
hatred will never let you face
the beast in man.
And one day, when you face this
beast alone, your courage intact,
your eyes kind,
out of your smile will bloom
a flower and those who love
you will behold you across ten
thousand worlds
of dying and birth.
Alone again
I'll go on
with bent head but knowing
the immortality of love
and on the long, rough road
both sun and moon will shine
lighting my way.

Chi Mai, I have spoken to groups in Rome, Palermo, Venice,
Bern, Zurich, Geneva, Lausanne, Biel, Paris, Liege, Brussels,
Amsterdam, Utrecht, Groningen, The Hague, Bremen, Bonn, Es-
sen, London, New York, Washington, D.C., and half the United
States, and I have told them, "When you want a product, you
have to give some money in order to have it. But when you want
the most precious things, like understanding and love in order to

end war and suffering, in order to help your friends who are struggling to end the war, you can only give what is most precious, and that is your own life. My sister did not commit suicide as many of you in the West think. No, my sister loved life. She had a good education and all the conditions to live a comfortable life, even in the midst of war. She wanted to offer the most precious thing a human being owns. That was her own life."

I speak with all my heart, and the number of people who understand and who join the struggle to end the war, to build a world based on understanding and love, grows bigger every day. However, those of us who resist the war machine must be patient and enduring in our efforts. Four years have passed since you left us, yet the blood and tears continue to flow, and I cannot rest. I carry with me photographs of the suffering to show to others, like the picture of Uncle Bay sitting in a corner of the pagoda with his head bent over, surrounded by seven small children. He wrote, "This is the fifth time my house has been destroyed. The first time was in Dau Tieng when my wife and I had just been married. The French came and burned down our house. I joined the resistance while my wife returned to the home of her mother. When we had finally, thatch by thatch, built a second home, it was bombed. Then, just after my wife gave birth to our youngest son, our house was destroyed, and we became refugees again. The fourth time my wife and her mother were killed by the bombs. I've been trying to raise seven children, like a rooster with seven chicks, and this is the fifth time we've lost a home. We moved to Saigon, but things are just as bad. How long must they go on fighting?"

Every day I speak at universities and meetings, and to the newspapers, radio, and television. Sometimes I speak seven or eight times in one day. The friends who organize for me are poor like our friends back home. Sometimes they even fast in order to have enough money to print appeals and rent halls for me to speak in. Some friends are afraid I will be too tired and they don't want to schedule so many engagements for me. But I insist, "I'm not tired, I'm not afraid of being tired. Let me speak! Schedule as much as you can." Because, Chi Mai, I am traveling very light. I have only photographs of you and photographs of our country's suffering as luggage. I must live and die with these pictures so that the children of Vietnam will one day sing songs of Peace.

With love from
your Sister,

Cao ngoc Phuong

---

[1]Thây is an informal title used for a teacher.

JOANNA MACY

In Indra's Net:
Sarvodaya & Our Mutual Efforts for Peace

DEPENDENT CO-ARISING

In examining social action from the Buddhist perspective, it is essential to stress *pratitya-samutpada* (Pali: *paticca-samuppada*), the Buddha's teaching of dependent co-arising. It is there that "the dynamics of transformation" are found. There is a deep inner connection between skillful, compassionate activity and the structure of life.

Action is not peripheral to wisdom. I am impatient with the notion that ethical action is something added on to reality, like so many "shoulds" and "oughts." In the Dharma there are no oughts. They disappear in the realization of dependent co-arising. Instead of commandments from on high, there is the simple, profound awareness that everything is interdependent and mutually conditioning—each thought, word, and act, and all beings, too, in the vast web of life. Once there is insight into that radical interdependence, certain ways of living and behaving emerge as intrinsic to it. Wisdom and morality, *prajña* and *sila*, are then seen as inseparable as two hands washing each other, to quote an early sutra. It is not one, then the other—they are simultaneous.

From the outset there is a deep moral thrust to the Dharma, rooted in the radical relativity of all phenomena. The Buddha's teaching of *anatman*, no-self, is one way of expressing *pratitya-samutdpada*, and it tells us that the "I," the ego, the sense that we exist as a separate entity, is actually a fiction. It is a convention, a useful one to be sure, but one to which we need not be in service. It is precisely because there is no self that needs to be defended, enhanced, improved, or even made more moral, that the realization of that truth releases us into action that is free from the burdens of selfhood. Not confined to the prison cell of the ego, we are liberated into those wider dimensions of life that are our true home.

This is not a burden that we nobly assume: "I am going out and save the world." That is very tedious, and the context for burning out. But when you experience it as being liberated into your true nature, which is inextricably interwoven with that of every other being, then your conceptual structure of reality and your response to it are inseparable. Each act becomes a way of affirming and knowing afresh the reality that the doctrine gives form to.

That also changes our notions of what detachment is and what power is. Many spiritual teachers and gurus preach a detachment that appears suspiciously akin to sublime indifference, as if one should or could remain aloof from the sufferings of others. In dependent co-arising, that is, in the last analysis, impossible; for we see ourselves as co-participating in the existence of all beings and in the world we co-create with them. Dharma detachment is from ego, not from the world.

In a hierarchical model of reality, which you find in mainstream Hinduism and Christianity for example, the ascent to pure Mind involves rising above phenomenality or the realm of *maya*. The real is equated with the changeless. Whether it is conceived as an immutable God or a Brahman above space and time, it is essentially and ontologically distinct from the apparent messiness and randomness of nature. In this view there is the temptation to escape from the disorderliness of "this" world to that changeless realm of pure order. The staggeringly bold move of the Buddha was to see that the real is what inheres in change rather than being removed from change; that it is found in the very dynamics of phenomenality. That is really the meaning of Dharma: the principles or "law" by which things change, the way things work. And that law—which the Buddha called Dharma and pratitya-samutpada (remember he said, "He who sees the Dharma sees dependent co-arising")—that law is such that every act we make, every word we speak, every thought we think is not only affected by the other elements in the vast web of being in which all things take part, but also has results so far-reaching that we cannot see or imagine them. We simply proceed with the act for its own worth, our sense of responsibility arising from our co-participation in all existence.

As the Buddha revealed, there is order, but it is not based on a timeless being. It had been assumed, and still is, that if there is order there must be that which orders it. There must be mind over and against nature, so to speak. But in pratitya-samutpada, life itself is its own order.

The same goes for what we construe power to be. In the patriarchal, hierarchical construction of reality, you have a one-way linear causality. We have been conditioned by that notion since Aristotle, and it has dominated both religion and science. Consequently power is seen as emanating from the top down. It is essentially power-over, and equated with domination, having one's way, pushing things around, becoming invulnerable to change. Such a notion of power requires defenses, whether of the ego or the nation-state.

But in dependent co-arising, causality is not linear; it is reciprocal. Power is a two-way street. It is not power-over, but power-with, where beings mutually affect and mutually enhance each other. The old linear notion is essentially that of a zero-sum game: the more you have the less I have. "You win, I lose." But that is breaking down as more and more people are talking about playing a "win-win game." That idea is very close to the systems notion of "synergy," which literally means power-with, and which requires no defenses because it operates through openness. This is the kind of power we find at play in an ecosystem or a neural net, where open reciprocal interaction is essential to skillful functioning and the arising of intelligence and beauty. It is also the power of the bodhisattva, of the "boundless heart" which opens in compassion and *muditha* to the griefs and joys in all beings.

We do not have a word for *muditha* in Western culture, probably because we have been conditioned by that top-down notion of power. It is the other side of *karuna* (compassion) and is one of the four abodes of the Buddha. Just as compassion is grief with the griefs of others, *muditha* is joy in the joy of others. It helps us identify with their gifts and resources, instead of feeling envious of them, which we tend to do when we view power as a zero-sum game. There are wonderful Buddhist meditations for developing the capacities for *karuna* and *muditha*. They are helpful and nourishing in undertaking social change work, and we often practice them in the despair and empowerment workshops.

Early Western scholars of Buddhism, beginning with Max Weber, have perceived Buddhism as "other-worldly" and without specific formulations of social ethics. They understood the release from this world as Buddhism's goal. Yet the Pali scriptures abound in passages where the Buddha deals explicitly with social ethics, and many more cases where the social implications are certainly obvious.

One of the great heroes of Buddhist tradition is King Asoka, who in his devotion to Dharma built hospitals and public wells and tree-lined roads for the "welfare of all beings." Historians recognize his efforts in the third century B.C.E. as the first public social service program in recorded history. This clearly reflects a distinctive character in Buddhism of honoring the phenomenal world. Shantideva, the great Indian Buddhist saint of the eighth century, saw service to others as the path leading to enlightenment, because it is precisely the capacity to give to another, even at the risk of your own well-being, that can take you into that no-space which is *anatman*, the transcendence of self. He found that selfless service can lead you into that experience more directly than just sitting in meditation. In our own times we have examples like the Unified Buddhist Church of Vietnam and the

Sarvodaya movement in Sri Lanka of Buddhists engaged in social action that is firmly grounded in the Buddhadharma.

SARVODAYA SHRAMADANA SANGAMAYA

The Sarvodaya movement started in Sri Lanka,[1] where in 1958, a Buddhist high school teacher named A. T. Ariyaratne took a handful of his students and started work camps in the poorest of outcaste villages. From that inconspicuous beginning grew a movement which has spread to over 5000 towns and villages and is now, as the largest non-governmental organization in the country, offering an alternative to the Western industrial model of development. Ariyaratne, inspired by Gandhian thought, adopted the name Sarvodaya for the movement. However, as a devout and learned Buddhist, he recast the notion in terms of the Buddhadharma, translating it as the "awakening of all." That is what the Buddha did under the Bo Tree: he woke up. And that is the movement's definition of what development is: not necessarily the transfer of technology or foreign aide schemes or steel mills or nuclear plants, but a "waking up" on every level—personal, spiritual, cultural, economic. A wholistic view of social change results, one which is deeply inspired by Buddhist teachings. Because of its extraordinary record in winning popular participation on the grassroots level, Sarvodaya has attracted the attention of development experts worldwide.

Sri Lanka is a beautiful country with very beautiful people, who are beset with the crushing problems endemic now to Third World societies—inflation, joblessness, deforestation, growing poverty, and hunger. In the Sarvodaya experience, Buddhism serves as a resource for social change. It is used to define what development is in terms that are meaningful to the people, and it offers community organizing strategies that release their energies and commitment.

Sarvodaya means "everybody waking up"—waking up to the degenerate condition of our village, waking up to work together and harness our energy, waking up to our capacity for compassion and joy and responsibility. The Four Noble Truths are even expressed in these terms, painted with illustrations on the walls on village centers: there is a decadent village, there is a cause for its misery, there is a hope for its regeneration, and there is a path. It is not expressed abstractly, but very concretely in terms of repaired roads, de-silted irrigation canals, nutrition programs, and schools. The Eightfold Path is even expressed architecturally. The movement's headquarters near Colombo is built on an octagonal plan around a large central courtyard with open prayer hall. The building on each side is named after an aspect of the path. The volunteers' hostel, for example, is in Right Action; the accounting office is in Right Mindfulness.

Most important of all, perhaps, is the notion and practice of "shramadana." Shramadana is how we wake up. The word means the sharing (*dana*) of human energy (*shrama*). The movement's full name, Sarvodaya Shramadana Sangamaya, literally means "the movement of everybody waking up by working together." Note the skillful means at work here in the use of the word *dana*. Generosity is the pre-eminent Buddhist virtue—in no other tradition is it accorded so central a position; but over the centuries *dana* had come to mean alms to the monks, the material support of the Buddhist Order. What the movement has done is to reclaim the original scope of *dana* and to present it, not just as alms-giving, but the gift of one's time, energy, skills, goods, and information to the community. So people "wake up" by giving.

I am convinced that a chief strength of the movement lies in the fact that it asks people what they can give rather than what they want to get—and provides them the opportunity to offer that in the shramadana camps. These are collective work projects which a village chooses and undertakes, such as cutting an access road, digging latrines, roofing the pre-school. In that context even the poorest families are expected to contribute, not only their labor but also food for the collective meal, and songs and ideas in the meetings. This is empowering to people. Even if it is only a betel leaf or matchbox of rice you can give, you walk differently on the earth as a bestower.

Another Buddhist teaching that is skillfully drawn upon is the four Brahma abodes, or as they subsequently became known, the four abodes of the Buddha: *metta, karuna, muditha,* and *upekkha,* or lovingkindness, compassion, joy in the joy of others, and equanimity. In the sutra in which this teaching appears, the Buddha is approached by someone who asks, "How can we enter Brahma's abode?" This was the goal of the Vedic people of his time and, up until then it was a question of the ritual sacrifices one performed and the ritual cleanliness one maintained. But the Buddha answered, "You can enter Brahma's abode right now; it is fourfold: just practice *metta, karuna, muditha,* and *upekkha* and you are in it."

The Sarvodaya movement takes these abodes very seriously and very engagingly as means and measure of being awake. They are translated, not just by clergy but by lay adults and children into day-to-day behavior in social enterprises in the village. *Metta* is the loving respect for all beings that gets you off your duff and · liberates you from self-involvement. Compassion is being out there, digging or dancing, to improve the common lot. *Muditha* is the pleasure you find in being of service, and equanimity keeps you going in spite of criticism and setbacks. These abodes are on the lips of every village organizer and painted on the walls of village centers. Every meeting, whether it is a village gathering or a committee on latrines, begins with two minutes of silence for *metta* meditation, extending loving thoughts to all beings.

The primary dictum of the Judeo-Christian tradition is to love your neighbor as yourself, but we are never told how to do it. It is not always easy to love people. It might be easy to love people in general, but how do you love someone you do not even like? The Buddhist tradition, with its high regard for means, for technique, teaches how to do this. These teachings can be lubricants and motivators to skillful personal and social change. Qualities like love and compassion are not just abstract virtues that are the property of saints and adepts. There are concrete ways by which anyone can experience these qualities in themselves. As the

Buddha said, "*Ehipassiko*," come and see. You don't have to be a Buddhist; come and see for yourself in your own experience.

In our workshops on despair and empowerment, we draw upon these teachings of the four abodes. There is a meditation practice for developing the quality of *metta* or lovingkindness, the first abode, which involves focusing on someone mentally and experiencing your desire that this person be free from fear, from greed, free from sorrow and the causes of suffering. Taking a moment to internally identify with your desire that another be free from suffering changes the whole ambiance of a conflicting relationship. It gives endurance and patience, and it releases our tremendous capacity for love.

The second abode, compassion, means to identify with the suffering of others, to experience their pain as your own. We are often reluctant to experience pain because we think we will fall apart, or we do not want to look at a problem unless we know the solution. Buddhism teaches that the first step is simply to experience the pain—we won't fall apart—and the ability to respond creatively and skillfully will arise naturally out of this openness. There is an exercise adapted from the Mahayana tradition that I share with people that we have found to be enormously helpful in this regard. It involves visualizing the suffering of the world coming in with the breath, passing through the nose, throat, lungs, and heart, and then out through the bottom of the heart back into the great net. You simply permit yourself to experience the pain, allowing it to pass through the heart and then letting it go. This is a very effective tool in opening to the compassion that inheres in us.

The third abode, joy in the joy of others, is a quality we tend to overlook. It is the flip side of compassion, and to the extent that you can experience the suffering of another as your own, you can also experience the joy and power and gifts of another as your own. The synergy that is inherent in dependent co-arising is made available through taking joy in the joy of others. The courage of Martin Luther King, Jr. or the endurance of Gandhi is not just Martin Luther King's or Gandhi's, but is ours too, by virtue of *anatman*, by virtue of the fact that we do not exist as separate beings but interpenetrate with all. We can draw on this imaginatively by seeing that the good done by any being, past or present, enters into this reality structure in which we exist, and constitutes an ever-present resource. Anyone with whom we come in contact—family, friends, the person next to you at the check-out counter—all have goodness and capacities that we can open to and share in. Looking at things this way helps release us from the envy and competitiveness which are such energy drains.

The fourth abode, *upekkha*, is usually translated as equanimity or impartiality, but those terms seem rather weak. As with the others, *upekkha* springs from the Jewel Net of Indra, the co-arising web in which we take being. This is an image from the *Avatamsaka Sutra*, in which reality is likened to a multi-dimensional net with each knot a jewel reflecting every other jewel.[2] As we regard another, we can let our consciousness sink within us like a stone, below the level of word and deed, to that deeper level of interdependent relationship. In each moment it arises in new forms, but the substratum of dynamic ordered unfolding of reality persists and sustains, and in it we can rest. Out of it we cannot fall. Below the separate "I's" that come like froth on the sea, that net is what we are, and in it we find the great peace.

The sense of deep trust and peace in the intertwining web of reality permits us to take risks, because we know we can never be separated from it. No stupidity or failure can sever us from it. Imprisonment, even death, cannot sever us from it. I am certain that our Vietnamese Buddhist sisters and brothers, who have worked so long for peace in their homeland in the face of violent repression, have been sustained and empowered by the deep peace of knowing that in the co-arising nature of things nothing that happens can sever them from the reality of that great peace, or from us.

Sarvodaya has taught me much about how spiritual teachings can inspire and guide people—Buddhist and non-Buddhist—in social action. Also, we can see in Sarvodaya that as well as empowering individuals in the work of social change, the Dharma gives direction to the change itself. The Buddha's teachings on economic sharing, political participation, right livelihood, and so forth, offer guidelines for building a sane, equitable, ecological, and nonviolent society. In reclaiming these teachings, Sarvodaya is creating a "social gospel" form of Buddhism.

Some fellow scholars of Buddhism, whom I had consulted, considered Sarvodaya's reinterpretation of doctrine—such as in its version of the four noble truths—to be a new-fangled adulteration of Buddhism, lacking doctrinal respectability. To present release from suffering in terms of irrigation, literacy, and marketing cooperatives appears to them to trivialize the Dharma. When I asked very learned Buddhist monks in Sri Lanka what they thought of this recasting of the four noble truths, I did so with the expectation that they, too, would see it as a corruption of the purity of the Buddha's teachings. Instead, almost invariably, they seemed surprised that a Buddhist would ask such a question— and gave an answer that was like a slight rap on the knuckles: "But it is the same teaching, don't you see? Whether you put it on the psycho-spiritual plane or on the socio-economic plane, there is suffering and there is cessation of suffering." In other words, you are not diluting or distorting the noble truths by applying them to conditions of physical misery or social conflict. Their truth lies in the contingent nature of suffering, however you view it. Because it has a cause, it can cease. Because it co-dependently arises, it can be overcome.

On Sarvodaya charts and murals, the Four Noble Truths are illustrated with wheels of causation featuring the interrelationship of disease, greed, and apathy, or between nutrition, literacy, *metta*, and self-reliance, for example. They reveal another way in which the notion of dependent co-arising is empowering to social action, because there is not one single cause you have to seek out and attack—be it malarial mosquitoes or local interest rates. Everything is so interrelated that whatever you do, whether you decide to organize a pre-school, a community kitchen, or a craft cooperative, each is equally valid. Each endeavor toward human well-being pulls a prop out from under the house of suffering.

I find that very applicable to social change here in North America. Whatever our contribution, it is of great value; we need not feel torn between responses to different aspects of the global crisis: "Oh, should I go out and try to protect the whales, or should I go and try to stop the strip-mining, or should I go march for disarmament at the U.N.?" If you simply stick with trying to stop the strip-mining, you're helping to save the whales, because it is all interwoven. And that is important to know if we are to stay sane and collected in our work, and if we are to respect and support each other. It helps us be more effective with other people, to assume that we are already working together.

By the same token, we become more effective by also assuming that we are all aware of the suffering and would like to stop it. When you intuit that everyone—to some extent, at least, and on some level of consciousness—feels pain for what is happening to our world, it changes your style. Your strategy and tactics become different. For example, our style in the anti-nuclear and peace movements has been largely predicated on the assumption that people do not know and do not care. So we come on to them with more and more terrifying information and an accusatory tone: "There are 50,000 nuclear missiles on hair-trigger alert— don't you realize where your tax dollars are going? Or how fast you would incinerate?" But when your point of departure is one of pre-existing interconnection—that is, when you assume that people hurt and care—the approach is different. It is one of opening—providing an opportunity, perhaps by just asking a question, that allows people to open to what they know in the depths of their being and have feared to acknowledge. What people most need to hear is not our information, but what is inside them already.

In the last analysis, what we are and what brought us into being is the Jewel Net of Indra. Co-arising and inseparable, we can never fall out of the web of our reality/home. Opening to its presence and resilience, we can now trust. Moving beyond ego fears, we can risk, we can act. Act, as the Buddha said, "bahujana hitaya bahujana sukhaya"—for the sake of all beings and for their happiness.

NOTES

[1]The idea of Sarvodaya originated in India with Gandhi. He evolved the Sanskrit word "Sarvodaya" to express John Ruskin's Christian-inspired idea of "Unto this Last," and he translated it as the "uplift or welfare of all."

[2]See *The Flower Ornament Scripture: A Translation of the Avatamsaka Sutra*, trans. Thomas Cleary, 3 volumes (Boston: Shambhala, 1984-1987).

CHRISTOPHER TITMUSS

Interactivity: Sitting for Peace and Standing for Parliament

May all beings abide in awareness,
may all beings abide in full attention,
may all beings engage in direct action.

I left the monkhood in Thailand in 1976. From there, I spent more time in Asia as a lay person, and a little time in Australia and the United States. I returned to England in May of 1977, a little more than ten years after I'd left. Until 1980, I had not taken much interest in political issues. I concentrated almost entirely on spiritual, psychological processes, integration and liberation of the human being. But on a flight to America in 1980, during the Reagan-Carter campaign, a connection between spirituality and political awareness was linked in my mind, quite spontaneously.

The first steps were particularly with women's issues, which had already begun to concern me, and I began to speak more with women in the women's movement. I also began to see the way that religion is hierarchical, patriarchal, and privilege-oriented; and how, in myself as a male, many things were taken for granted. For a simple example, in most places in the world, I wouldn't give a thought about going out for a walk at night. This kind of privilege.

As this political awareness began to take place, it went to a very keen interest in Marx. I felt a genuine moral concern from him, true insights of a philosophical, social, and economic nature. He had a great passion and a ruthless intellect with regard to the social reality. Of course there were shortcomings in his thinking: insufficient knowledge and understanding of the situation of women, a lack of ecological awareness, and a lack of attention to psychological processes. I began to associate myself with what I was calling "the politics of protest." That included giving a peace workshop, bringing up peace issues on retreats, and giving support to such groups as the Greenham Common peace camps, CND, Friends of the Earth, and the Green Party.

When speaking to retreatants, I emphasize the need for compassionate action. I feel that amongst meditators in all the Buddhist traditions there is too much passivity, which needs to be balanced with a greater outer awareness. The bridge between inner and outer awareness is direct action, although that may take a variety of expressions. Some people take direct action in the immediacy of their living situation. For instance, at home one can be aware of seeing something clearly and directly responding to it, an expression of love and understanding. Then there are social, spiritual, and political issues which require direct action. I see among meditators a certain reluctance to become involved with groups which are involved in direct action, a hesitancy to take responsibility in this area.

In the past few years, though, this has begun to change, so that there is a greater sense coming about that the inner and outer are not really separate. I feel this awareness is very, very important. More and more meditators are becoming involved in major issues affecting this planet. I hear of more friends who are going to prison, who are leafletting, who are involved with groups which are socially and politically active. Equally important, people who are already involved in direct action are coming to retreats, and therefore are giving consideration to their inner selves as well as what is happening out in the world. This combination of people from the outside coming to retreats and people from the inside going to the outside means that there is more and more bridging taking place. Both are giving more and more support to each other and the genuine liberation of both people and planet.

I feel that it is this combination of the inner and the outer which gives the sustaining factor to social and political awareness. Some of the groups which have a long-term commitment to social/political changes tend to have a strong spiritual background. The Quakers immediately come to mind. When political groups lack spiritual background one of two things seems to happen. One, there is burnout (as we saw with so many people from the '60's and the anti-Vietnam era) and two, there is a gradual increase of anger in the mind. This brings about more division within groups who are basically in agreement, more sectarianism and more narrow-mindedness. So what results is either burnout or aggression. But when there is some kind of inner awareness or spiritual foundation for one's action, there is less likelihood of these two occurring as a result of direct action.

People are beginning to see that personal pain and global pain are not two separate factors, but very much interrelated. Some people experience inside of themselves what they conceive of as being the pain of the world, but in a way it's the pain of themselves. There are others who experience inside of themselves what they conceive of as being purely personal pain. In a way, it's the pain of the world.

I feel there is a change taking place, that the area of pain is beginning to have another kind of significance. People who have engaged in a meditative awareness begin to see pain as a motivating factor, a reason to work on themselves and issues rather than as something which is life-denying.

Meditation can help us deal with living in a world where direct action exposes us to intimidation and terror. These days I am getting invitations to give workshops in which I relate the practice specifically to aggression in all the forms that it can take. In England at the present time, training workshops in nonviolent direct action are taking place all over the country. I was in one of them myself. Exercises are used. For example, half the group will be the policemen, and the other half will be the people engaged in a sitting protest. The police will move in, arms locked, pushing the protestors against the wall. We reproduce the boot going into the shin, the treading on toes, the dragging of people across the floor on their backs, which is very painful, and the policemen walking over women's breasts. All this goes on, which the camera never sees in these kinds of protests. It touches off fear and anger in the protestors. Some workshop participants are afraid of losing these feelings. There's a belief in nonviolence, yet in reality, under pressure, violence comes up inside of oneself and one wants to react against those who inflict pain. For instance, during a march, people are shouting out abuse, putting the protestors down, or occasionally, there is stone throwing. In spite of nonviolence, the anger comes up because it is latent inside. With the recognition of latent anger, more people want to work on the aggression and violence they experience. It seems to me that meditation has a real contribution to make to the peace movement in this area. Through exercises in self-awareness, we can feel the pressure and aggression and learn to work with the pain, to observe it and go into it, but to not feel threatened by it.

Moreover, many of the people in the peace movement who consider themselves to be without religion in any form, who see themselves as humanistic, secular, and who cherish those values, do not feel that their personal values are threatened in any way by meditation practice. In addition, it is not an hierarchical model we are using. The first generation of insight meditation (*vipassana*) teachers working in the West are pretty much Westerners. Instead of a hierarchical model we are based much more in friendship. This also contributes to allowing new people to feel comfortable in coming to do meditative practice. So people in the peace movement can use meditation practice to do exercises in which they experience pressure and aggression, to discuss aggression and to work on themselves.

In London we gave a workshop for about 15 people. We basically got people to talk about their feelings—what actually comes up when they are involved in threatening situations. This is a really major step, to say, "Yes, this is what's going on in me," just to acknowledge the terror and the fury. That, in itself, is half the process. I gave a talk about ways and means of working with those feelings. Then we just engaged in exercises representing peace activities. I put the emphasis on "sitting for peace," "standing for peace," and "lying down for peace" and on the effort to keep still and keep relaxed, even in the face of aggression. Their own pain, which arises in their bodies, becomes a motivating force. We work with seeing how well the mind can relax and keep it together despite the fact that pain is occurring.

Buddhists have a great resource to bring to nonviolence training. One of Buddhism's transcendent virtues is the upholding of a nonviolent view towards life; and maintaining that as clearly and as carefully as possible with regard to all forms of life. Certainly the Buddhist Peace Fellowship can do a tremendous job because the Dharma really goes deep. I think that is the potency of the Dharma; it tries to work with the root of things, and sees that nonviolence is not just something that one applies in a peace march but it is that sensitivity with regard to the way one treats creatures, the way one makes choices in a supermarket. Our Buddhist background and training and wisdom says that nonviolence is a day-to-day experience.

Now that message has not yet reached the peace movement. Yet within the peace movement, as within the culture at large, there is a growing recognition that we are all interconnected. It is a growing sense of the systemic unity of all life, reflected in the "Gaia Hypothesis" and even in our fears of extinction through environmental destruction or nuclear holocaust. What we need are practices to help us perceive and experience this "interactivity." In vipassana practice, when settling into deep clarity, we see progressively the interactivity of mind and body, and of ourselves and the rest of the cosmos. As the Buddha said time and time again, for anything to arise, there must be conditions for its arising. That means that it is dependently arising. Everything is related to everything else. Nothing has its own unique self-existence. The awareness of this interconnectedness brings us a sense with regard to life. Through this awareness one wishes to contribute to life, to the way life really is—interconnected, interrelated, unity. One sees again and again, and that is where the observation factor comes in, the way the mind influences the body, the body influences the mind, the way one influences the world and the world influences one. Everything keeps expressing its interrelationship, its interactivity, again and again. The lack of a center or essence is really the key to wisdom, compassion, and liberation.

One of the fundamental aspects of conventional politics is that there is opposition, and all the aggression and negative angry reaction which accompanies it. "We are right, they are wrong. We know, they don't know." A spiritual-political awareness needs to come from another position entirely, something like, "Look at what we've made of our world. Look at the condition it's in. We have to explore together new ways." In some respects, this framework is based on the Chinese proverb, "He or she who attacks another, defeats himself or herself."

The Chernobyl tragedy, in April 1987, was a turning point for me. I had been a member of the Green Party, which I would say is tremendously in tune with the Dharma and spiritual awareness. It is almost an outer expression of it. I very much appreciated the care and concern of the people involved in it. In May, we were having a meeting to decide who should stand for Parliament for the Green Party in the next general election from our constituency. Two or three days before, I had been talking to friends, receiving calls from the continent, discussing concerns about Chernobyl. One friend said, "It's obvious. You've got to be the one to stand." So at the meeting, there were about 20 participants, and my name was put forward, and I received a unanimous vote. So I said, "Well, right, let's do it."

Why electoral politics? For me, education, direct action, and electoral politics amount to the same. One of my abiding interests is the communication of Dharma, dealing with the realities of life in a caring way, especially to people who have no connection with it, for whom it is like listening to a foreign language. The end result—becoming a member of Parliament—is not what is primary, although of course it is present. Rather, as in good

Dharma practice, it is the here-and-now situation of active and hopefully effective communication. There is also a very great energy to explore ways and means by which we can be engaged in direct action. We communicate issues to educate people in the best sense of education, which is to uplift their awareness, so that they understand that politics is not just voting every few years, it is to be expressed in daily life. And so we're doing those things also.

There are of course some dangers in becoming socially engaged as a Buddhist. The main danger, as with all things, is the ego becoming increasingly involved in the act. This ego very easily begins to identify itself around the issue, and a certain moralistic attitude, a certain self-righteousness and seeing things too simplistically comes about. This can come out in the form of a really one-sided view, in very heavy judgements. For example, some people view some political leaders as though they are completely without scruples, just filled with aggression, rage, ill will, rather than seeing that their motives include a real concern for people and a desire to protect them, although they may use ways we find questionable. If we do not see where the other person is coming from, self-righteousness, aggression, arrogance, and positing oneself as knowing or special can come up.

The other great danger, one which the Green Party in Germany is having great difficulty with, is how easily compromise arises in order to make inroads. One starts up with certain principles and then one compromises, compromises, and finally, one has lost one's integrity. But wherever there are dangers, there are safeguards. There are two safeguards here. Firstly, self-observation. Once one gets so involved that one stops looking at oneself, I think it's time to forget political work. The second is that one must have honesty from one's friends. Actual clear feedback. As the Buddha said, "A friend is not somebody who flatters. A friend is someone who is honest." That outer awareness, so that there is feedback and the responsibility to be receptive to it, and self-observation are the safeguards against the dangers of engaged Buddhism.

Dharma humor is another important safeguard—being able to step back and laugh at ourselves, laugh at our arrogance and be able to see it. Politics is often so serious. Of course there are serious issues, but there is a healthy response in humor and the ability to laugh at oneself and to connect in that way.

To me, compassion is not a feeling, it is an action. There are many ways in which people can further integrate practice with social and political awareness and action. I think three things are essential. The first one is collective cooperation with others. The individual, in the face of global and social events, is virtually powerless. So that means going out and meeting with people who are concerned—getting out of one's front door on a miserable winter's night and going to a meeting which is attended by three or four people. The second is to be thoroughly informed, not just to look at things simplistically and have a judgment. The third is, "What else is there to do? What else is important?"

JUDITH RAGIR

Rape

On a rainy, summer afternoon a few years ago, just two days after *sesshin*,[1] I was pushed into my car in a Chicago alley and
raped. My husband and I spent an unbearable afternoon looking
for the violator, to no avail. The police said that they would not
investigate the case unless I agreed to prosecute the rapist, and I
said, "Yes, I will prosecute."

Morally and socially, rape is an abomination. But there is no easy
answer to the question of what to do about it or even how to
come to grips with the facts of rape, war, and other atrocities of
society. The questions and solution to the problems of violence in
our global society are complicated. In some Middle Eastern societies in olden times, it was simple: castrate the rapist. Could it be
so simple in modern times? Is jailing a rapist going to bring about
a more peaceful world?

I now see rape as clearly a violent/power act, not a sexual
one. My over-riding fear is the moment of force at the beginning
of the experience, more than the actual sexual act. It seems odd
to me that the sexual aspect is what most people seem to respond
to. If I had just been mugged, they would not have been so concerned. But for me, the fear is the moment of violence more than

the sex. Still, being raped is the ultimate act of intrusion and disrespect.

I wrote the following as an expression of how I coped
personally and spiritually with an act of violence against myself.
In that sense, the writing is more about Buddhist attitude than a
social position about rape. The amazing thing, which I have tried
to capture in this writing, is that my Buddhist practice clearly
gave me the staff with which to walk through this experience. I
actually was able to convert this catastrophe into an effective tool
for my personal and spiritual growth.

RAPE: 1

I will not take this out on myself
I will not kill myself
after the invasion of this man
I refuse to turn against myself
and as I refuse
the anger goes outward.
I pound the sofa, pound and pound.
I kick my legs like a mad child,
no, no, no!
I will not do what He wants
devastate myself
("Have I hurt your pride?" he asks, that son-of-a-bitch)
I pound the shit out of him on the sofa.
My hands turn into knives.
I realize
I am stabbing *him.*

Yet all the insidious ways come out.
I overeat to punish myself.
I eat the feelings down instead of letting them ooze out
     of my pores
out my fiery, demonic eyes.
Why is a woman too pretty

for demonic eyes?
It's not ladylike to pound and pound
and yet I will not eat myself alive.
He is the culprit
He should eat *himself* alive, *he* self-destruct.

Thank God, I at least screamed for "Help!" in the
    beginning.
That I tried to defend myself, at least a little.
It hurts the most, this lack of defense,
this passivity and compliance of surrendering
thinking he would kill me.
Something so strong in me mourns,
wishes I could have protected myself
fought for my rights.

Hurl these spitballs of fire out!
I am not a compliant little girl
I am a screaming redhead with demonic eyes
and Knives coming out of my hands
and muscles bulging out my arms
who pounds and pounds him
until his death.

RAPE: 2

He pushed me into the car from behind,
I was screaming,
I sat in the middle of a man and boy, surrounded
they kept pushing my head down so my chin touched
    my chest
"Don't you look at me. Don't you look at me or I'll kill
    you"
over and over his mantra.
They pulled at my rings.

I took off my diamond wedding ring and gave it to
    them.
It was raining out and it was afternoon,
but instead I was under the full moon sitting zazen in
    the country
as I was just two nights before.
I thought in a flash of a second
this story:

THE MOON CANNOT BE STOLEN

Ryokan, a Zen master, lived the simplest kind of life in a little
hut at the foot of a mountain. One evening a thief visited the
hut only to discover there was nothing in it to steal.

Ryokan returned and caught him. "You may have come a
long way to visit me," he told the prowler, "and you should
not return empty-handed. Please take my clothes as a gift." The
thief was bewildered. He took the clothes and slunk away.

Ryokan sat naked, watching the moon. "Poor fellow," he
mused, "I wish I could give him this beautiful moon."[2]

To go towards the enemy, no resistance
to go towards and merge with the object and therefore
    to lose the subject
These things I had contemplated fully the week before
    at sesshin
at Catching the Moon Mountain Monastery.
In the middle of this horrible commotion,
still calm from sesshin,
I tried to go towards my enemy, even in rape.
To the ordinary mind, this is heresy,
This is the guilt that I didn't defend myself.
But who is there to defend?
only to become fully the situation
a woman amidst a violent crime,
where passivity and compliance gets her out alive.
I tried to stay in the center now
to realize the impermanence of the horrific situation

one breath after the next breath
through the tunnel of this trap
until I was out.
So I couldn't see what direction he left in,
He made me kiss the front seat,
I knew it was over,
my heart pounding.
to go towards my victim
my oppressor as victim
I felt so deeply his suffering.
to go towards my oppressor's suffering
to become suffering
to be, simply in the action of the crime without
    judgment
I came out alive.

Who can be ungrateful or not respectful
Even to senseless things,
Not to speak of man?
Even though he may be a fool,
Be warm and compassionate toward him.
If by any chance he should turn against me
and become a sworn enemy
and abuse and persecute me,
I should sincerely bow down with humble language
In reverent belief that He is
The merciful avatar of Buddha,
who used devices to emancipate me
From sinful Karma
That has been produced and accumulated
Upon myself
By my own egoistic delusions and attachment
Through the countless cycles of Kalpa.[3]

Now two weeks later there are many
supposed-to's of hate.
I do not have the ordinary world's reaction

I think of and understand for the first time
this story:

NANSEN CUTS THE CAT IN TWO

Nansen saw the monks of the eastern and western halls fighting over a cat. He seized the cat and told the monks: "If any of
you say a good word, you can save the cat." No one answered.
So Nansen boldly cut the cat in two pieces.

That evening Joshu returned and Nansen told him about
this. Joshu removed his sandals and, placing them on his head,
walked out. Nansen said: "If you had been there, you could
have saved the cat."
Commentary:
Had Joshu been there,
He would have enforced the edict oppositely,
Joshu snatches the sword
and Nansen begs for his life.[4]

I did not know then that this
violator
would turn the world around
that the rapist would set my mind free.

or

that My Anger would kill him
pounding and stabbing
my empty couch
at midnight.

Everything is in reverse.
I see in one of Frida Kahlo's paintings
that the roots of a tree are coming out of a skeleton
    buried in its soil
death fertilizing life
as this rape nourishes my understanding
and suffering teaches our souls.

But this is so upside-down to ordinary mind.
How dare I say, in ordinary mind,
the rape is a gift
and yet
Zap! the hit of *kyosaku*
I understand
something.

I had been saying all winter
that the structure of my ego-building
had finally collapsed
and it was laying
in ruin and rubble
in the floor of my pelvis.
Head, shoulders, ribcage, spine, collapsed in a pile.
and now I say,
Zap,
like a vacuum cleaner,
the rape sucking all the debris out
and spinning it with great force into the universe
clean and empty inside
Where is the person who got raped?

RAPE: 3

Seven weeks later. Today I didn't go to the studio to get the
equipment. I realized that it was the repeat of the situation of the
rape: parking the car in the alley, running up to get something
and then the fear of that moment of getting pushed into the car. I
decided to wait until someone could help me. I didn't like that I
was still afraid. I don't talk about it much any more but sometimes
it peeps out of me. "Did you know that I still think about it every
day, often many times a day?" I ask a friend. Sometimes when I'm
alone, I'll just cry and then realize this sadness and vulnerability
is the shock wave. I still constantly look around me in every direction when I'm on the city streets, especially at night. When I

go to the zendo in the dark of the early morning, I look in every doorway and check the back seat of the car. I dream of fending off attackers, and everywhere I go for support, there is none. Sometimes when I'm talking to myself, this light blue, very soft voice will come up and tell me of her fears, weaknesses, and her needs for lots and lots of comfort. I know I've never learned to nurture myself enough. I have kept up my obligations and worldly duties, but, inside, I have been totally rearranged.

This rearrangement I've been calling a realization, which it is. Though I cannot pinpoint exactly what has changed in me, I know that I am different. I think the greatest realization of the whole experience was to see my spiritual practice in action. It succeeded in stabilizing me through this traumatic experience. "Spiritual Stability," my teacher calls it. I saw that the years of practice are built into my life; that I could not internally collapse, which would lead, perhaps, into an extended depression. Doing what I always do on a daily basis, I tried to maintain the most wholesome attitude of mind I could. There is nowhere to go. My friend writes me, "I wonder what the experience of your rapist was. It reminds me of when the Sixth Patriarch was pursued by his enemy, and he simply gave over the robe and bowl. The enemy is deeply moved by such resignation. But that state of mind has to exist before the attack, not intellectually, but *really*.

I felt for the first time a true sensibility of the Three Treasures: the Buddha, the Dharma, and the Sangha. Each in its own way made a web of support I could fall into like a net under a tightrope walker. I really felt that I took refuge in the Buddha, Dharma, Sangha, for I certainly could not walk through that experience alone. In many ways, my ordinary mind could not support the fact of rape. I was unwired. Only the Buddha realm as expressed by the Dharma could give me an attitude of mind that could embrace rape, and only through the love of the Sangha could I have the strength, will, love, and comfort to shed my ego and walk my path through this experience. To take refuge is "to retreat into a shelter that is safe from danger," and, because of a continuous practice, I did have access to the Triple Treasure. I surprised myself. I did act according to the belief that every experience is a powerful teacher, and I did transform, combust, move the energies of this negative experience.

NOTES

[1]*Sesshin* - a 7-day Zen meditation retreat.

[2]Paul Reps, *Zen Flesh Zen Bones* (Rutland, Vermont: Charles E. Tuttle Co., 1957), p. 27.

[3]Excerpted from the Bodhisattva's vow by Torei Zenji, from *Sutra Book for Dai Bosatsu Zendo Kongo-ji and the New York Zendo Shobo-ji* (New York: Zen Studies Society, 1976).

[4]Reps, *Op. Cit.*, p. 128.

CHARLENE SPRETNAK

Dhamma at the Precinct Level

The goals of social-change activism have changed. The single-issue campaigns that emerged in the seventies have become overlapping fields from which a new politics is growing. Now it is understood that peace in an ecological wasteland, or life on an ecologically restored continent with great social injustice, or a perfectly decentralized economy with patriarchal, violent ways of being are glaringly inadequate goals. Now it is understood that we as a species must teach ourselves to be nonviolent or there will be no age beyond the nuclear age. We must drop the hubris of pretending that we live on top of nature and learn to interact with the earth *on its own terms*. We must restructure institutions in scale and function so that people have greater control over their lives—and so that the despoilers of this blue-green planet are not permitted to pollute it with toxic wastes and artificial life forms before they blithely move on to space colonies with their impervious can-do bravado. When has the need for wisdom and compassion ever been greater than at this postmodern moment in history?

The gospel of modernity promised prosperity and happiness in exchange for unqualified industrial growth, no matter what the cost to the Earth community. Surrounded now by toxic waste dumps, military tensions over "resources," broken communities, and a despoiled planet, we seek—with a paradoxical mixture of patience and urgency—a new frame of reference, a new mode of living on the Earth, a new politics. Green politics has sprung up in countries around the world as an evolving response to the interlinked crises. In the United States, Greens have delineated ten key values of the movement: ecological wisdom, grassroots democracy, personal and social responsibility, nonviolence, decentralization, community-based economics, postpatriarchal values, respect for diversity (including religious pluralism), global responsibility, and future focus.

The grand sweeping scope and comprehensive goals aside, however, for Buddhists, like many others, the ends do not justify any means. *What you get is how you do it.* Each thought—and the attendant action, if there is one—plants the seed of a future thought. Hatred, greed, delusion, violence, fear, revenge will bring forth one kind of future. Peacefulness, equanimity, lovingkindness, patience, compassion, and wisdom will bring forth another.

When Buddhists get off the meditation cushion to get their hands dirty with nitty-gritty political work, they encounter the same kinds of frustrations, disputes, and psychodramas as everyone else. Sometimes they cause them.

Suppose a Buddhist meditator is working in a social-change group, a local chapter of a national organization or perhaps an entirely local or regional effort. Someone in the group has behaved badly toward the Buddhist on several occasions, usually in covert ways, and his or her antagonism shows no signs of letting up. Splendid! Here's a chance to put meditation practice into action.

If the group is composed entirely of Buddhist meditators, the two parties share some crucial assumptions. They both regard ill will, jealousy, hatred, and seething rage as defilements that arise in the mind. If those unskillful mind states are fed, the mental chain reaction will continue to grow; if they are observed with skillful awareness, the chain reaction will be broken and the mind will be purified. Because the Buddhist meditators do not

want defilements in their own minds and because they consider
it a transgression to disturb anyone's peacefulness, they both want
to work to avoid the interpretations and actions that encourage
the unskillful mind states. With right effort, they will probably
succeed.

But let's be realistic. The odds are extremely slim that a social-
change group—unless it's the Buddhist Peace Fellowship—is
composed entirely of Buddhist meditators. Perhaps the Buddhist's antagonistic colleague has a spiritual practice of some
sort, though, so that both persons are working within a context
that values lovingkindness over the tedious tantrums of ego.
More likely, the antagonist's mind is tormented with agitation,
fear, hatred, jealousy, and delusion. In a desperate attempt to triumph over his or her insecurities, the antagonist attacks, under-
mines, and shuns various people. The ruse is transparent to
nearly all onlookers, but still he or she continues. There is little
choice; the mind is trapped. The antagonist interprets any kindness as a show of weakness and doggedly seeks the jagged satisfaction of revenge or one-up-man-ship. Still, the Buddhist activist
and the destructive—or perhaps just obnoxious—activist must
work together repeatedly. After all, they live in the same town
and both are particularly concerned with peace issues, or ecology, or community-based economics, or Green politics, or whatever.

A dismal situation. *What would the Buddha do?*

Wearing a modest array of "Question Authority," "No Nukes,"
and "Animal Rights" buttons on his robes, the Buddha would no
doubt come to the next political meeting and generate such
strong *metta* (lovingkindness) toward the troubled mind that
feelings of deep peacefulness and good will would arise within
the antagonist, freeing him or her, perhaps for the first time, from
consuming rage and self-hatred, making tangible as *experiential
knowledge* mindstates of love, harmony, and gratitude to the wondrous web of life.

Can our grassroots Buddhist activist pull this off? Alas, not
likely. What then? A thin veneer of wimpy *metta* overlying
stockpiles of reactive ill will would be extremely off-putting and

counterproductive, no better than a glazed expression of New Age smotherlove.

The path of right effort here is clear. Our Buddhist must demonstrate in the political work right action and right speech, must keep the precepts of morality, and must end the daily meditation with *metta* for the antagonist and all beings. Our Buddhist will sometimes take a tumble—but with awareness!— noting mentally, for instance, "Exasperation is arising in my mind—because of the comprehensive idiocy of that person's proposal! I observe exasperation!" And a few moments later: "OK, OK, I observe anger and reactive negativity based on past ego wounds." (If the antagonist were bullying or otherwise victimizing others, the Buddhist would, of course, step in with such strong words as might be necessary, delivered from an active rather than reactive mind, but let's assume that this is not the case).

With right effort, the process carries the day. The *metta* becomes deeper and stronger. The antagonist and others notice that the Buddhist is centered, less carelessly reactive than most people, and usually active with clarity and ease but without pretension. The situation is awkward but workable.

Projects are completed. Membership ebbs and flows across the lines of various single-issue campaigns over the years. Sometimes the Buddhist and the antagonist find themselves thrown together at an event or during work on a campaign, but as it happens, not again for any period as long as their initial encounter. It seems as if nothing has happened.

Then one day the Buddhist hears surprising news: the antagonist and a couple of others from the old political group have begun a practice of Buddhist meditation! Reportedly, they have become more at ease, less unhappy.

Too far-fetched? This has happened many times in many places. For Dhamma is greater than its messengers. One sees with amazement over time that a life lived in Dhamma, even imperfectly, is the greatest effort one can make for a better tomorrow. Dhamma, the great transformer, has everything to do with transformational politics—and nothing at all.

JOANNA MACY

Taking Heart:
Spiritual Exercises for Social Activists

To heal our society, our psyches must heal as well. The military, social, and environmental dangers that threaten us do not come from sources outside the human heart; they are reflections of it, mirroring the fears, greeds, and hostilities that separate us from ourselves and each other. For our sanity and our survival, therefore, it appears necessary to engage in spiritual as well as social change, to merge the inner with the outer paths. But how, in practical terms, do we go about this?

Haunted by the desperate needs of our time and beset, as many of us are, by more commitments than we can easily carry, we can wonder where to find the time and energy for spiritual disciplines. Few of us feel free to take to the cloister or the zafu to seek personal transformation.

Fortunately, we do not need to withdraw from the world, or spend long hours in solitary prayer or meditation, to begin to wake up to the spiritual power within us. The activities and encounters of our daily lives can serve as the occasion for that kind of discovery. I would like to share some simple exercises that can permit that to happen.

I often share these mental practices in the course of my workshops. Participants who have found them healing, energizing, and easy to use in their daily activities have urged me to make them more widely available. I have been reluctant to put them in writing; they are best shared orally, in personal interaction. This is especially true of these forms of what I call "social mysticism," where the actual physical presence of fellow human beings is used to help us break through to deeper levels of spiritual awareness.

The four exercises offered here—on death, compassion, mutual power, and mutual recognition—happen to be adapted from the Buddhist tradition. As part of our planetary heritage, they belong to us all. No belief system is necessary, only a readiness to attend to the immediacy of one's own experiencing. They will be most useful if read slowly with a quiet mind (a few deep breaths help), and if put directly into practice in the presence of others.

MEDITATION ON DEATH

Most spiritual paths begin with the recognition of the transiency of human life. Medieval Christians honored this in the mystery play of *Everyman*. Don Juan, the yaqui sorcerer, taught that the enlightened warrior walks with death at his shoulder. To confront and accept the inevitability of our dying releases us from attachments and frees us to live boldly—alert and appreciative.

An initial meditation on the Buddhist path involves reflection on the two-fold fact that "death is certain" and "the time of death, uncertain." In our world today, the thermonuclear bomb, serving in a sense as a spiritual teacher, does that meditation for us, for we all know now that we can die together at any moment, without warning. When we deliberately let the reality of that possibility surface in our consciousness, it can be painful, of course, but it also helps us rediscover some fundamental truths about life. It jolts us awake to life's vividness, its miraculous quality as something given unearned, heightening our awareness of its beauty and the uniqueness of each object, each being.

As an occasional practice in daily life: Look at the person you en-counter (stranger or friend), Let the realization arise in you that this person may die in a nuclear war. Keep breathing. Observe that face, unique, vulnerable...those eyes still can see; they are not empty sock-ets...the skin is still intact...Become aware of your desire, as it arises, that this person be spared such suffering and horror, feel the strength of that desire...keep breathing...Let the possibility arise in your con-sciousness that this may be the person you happen to be with when you die...that face the last you see...that hand the last you touch..it might reach out to help you then, to comfort, to give water. Open to the feelings for this person that surface in you with the awareness of this possibility. Open to the levels of caring and connection it reveals in you.

BREATHING THROUGH

Our time assails us with painful information about threats to our future and the present suffering of our fellow beings. We hear and read of famine, torture, poisonous wastes, the arms race, an-imals and plants dying off. Out of self-protection, we all put up some degree of resistance to this information; there is fear that it might overwhelm us if we let it in, that we might shatter under its impact or be mired in despair. Many of us block our aware-ness of the pain of our world because our culture has conditioned us to expect instant solutions: "I don't think about nuclear war (or acid rain) because there is nothing I can do about it." With the value our society places on optimism, our contemplations of such fearful problems can cause us to feel isolated, and even a bit crazy. So we tend to close them out—and thereby go numb.

Clearly, the distressing data must be dealt with if we are to respond and survive. But how can we do this without falling apart? In my own struggle with despair, it seemed at first that I had to either block out the terrible information or be shattered by it. I wondered if there wasn't a third alternative to going numb or going crazy. The practice of "breathing through" helped me find it.

Basic to most spiritual traditions, as well as to the systems view of the world, is the recognition that we are not separate, isolated entities, but integral and organic parts of the vast web of life. As such, we are like neurons in a neural net, through which flow currents of awareness of what is happening to us, as a species and as a planet. In that context, the pain we feel for our world is a living testimony to our interconnectedness with it. If we deny this pain, we become like blocked and atrophied neurons, deprived of life's flow and weakening the larger body in which we take being. But if we let it move through us, we affirm our belonging; our collective awareness increases. We can open to the pain of the world in confidence that it can neither shatter nor isolate us, for we are not objects that can break. We are resilient patterns within a vaster web of knowing.

Because we have been conditioned to view ourselves as separate, competitive, and therefore fragile entities, it takes practice to relearn this kind of resilience. A good way to begin is by practicing simple openness, as in the exercise of "breathing through," adapted from an ancient Buddhist meditation for the development of compassion.

Relax. Center on your breathing . . . visualize your breath as a stream flowing up through your nose, down through windpipe, lungs. Take it down through your lungs and, picturing a hole in the bottom of your heart, visualize the breath-stream passing through your heart and out through that hole to reconnect with the larger web of life around you. Let the breath-stream, as it passes through you, appear as one loop within that vast web, connecting you with it . . . keep breathing . . .

Now open your awareness to the suffering that is present in the world. Drop for now all defenses and open to your knowledge of that suffering. Let it come as concretely as you can . . . concrete images of your fellow beings in pain and need, in fear and isolation, in prisons, hospitals, tenements, hunger camps . . . no need to strain for these images, they are present to you by virtue of our interexistence. Relax and just let them surface, breathe them in . . . the vast and countless hardships of our fellow humans, and of our animal brothers and sisters as well, as they swim the seas and fly the air of this ailing planet. Breathe in that pain like a dark stream, up through your nose, down through your trachea, lungs and heart, and out again into the world net . . . you are asked to do nothing for now, but let it pass through your heart . . . keep breathing . . . be sure that stream flows through and out again; don't hang on to the pain . . . surrender it for now to the healing resources of life's vast web . . .

With Shantideva, the Buddhist saint, we can say, "Let all sorrows ripen in me." We help them ripen by passing them through our hearts . . . making good, rich compost out of all that grief . . . so we can learn from it, enhancing our larger, collective knowing . . .

If you experience an ache in the chest, a pressure within the rib cage, that is all right. The heart that breaks open can contain the whole universe. Your heart is that large. Trust it. Keep breathing.

This guided meditation serves to introduce the process of breathing through, which, once experienced, becomes useful in daily life in the many situations that confront us with painful information. By breathing through the bad news, rather than bracing ourselves against it, we can let it strengthen our sense of belonging in the larger web of being. It helps us remain alert and open, whether reading the newspaper, receiving criticism, or simply being present for a person who is suffering.

For activists working for peace and justice, and those dealing most directly with the griefs of our time, the practice helps prevent burnout. Reminding us of the collective nature of both our problems and our power, it offers a healing measure of humility. It can also save us from self-righteousness. For when we can take in our world's pain, accepting it as the price of our caring, we can let it inform our acts without needing to inflict it as a punishment on others who are, at the moment, less involved.

THE GREAT BALL OF MERIT

Compassion, which is grief in the grief of others, is but one side of the coin. The other side is joy in the joy of others—which in Buddhism is called *muditha*. To the extent that we allow ourselves to identify with the sufferings of other beings, we can identify with their strengths as well. This is very important for our own sense of adequacy and resilience, because we face a time of great challenge that demands of us more commitment, endurance and courage than we can ever dredge up out of our individual supply. We can learn to draw on the other neurons in the net, and to view them, in a grateful and celebrative fashion, as so much "money in the bank."

The concept here resembles the Christian notion of grace. Recognizing our own limitations, we cease to rely solely on individual strength and open up to the power that is beyond us and can flow through us. The Buddhist "Ball of Merit" is useful in helping us see that this power or grace is not dependent upon belief in God, but operates as well through our fellow beings. In so doing, it lets us connect with each other more fully and appreciatively than we usually do. It is most helpful to those of us who have been socialized in a competitive society, based on a win-lose notion of power. "The more you have, the less I have." Conditioned by that patriarchal paradigm of power, we can fall prey to the stupidity of viewing the strengths or good fortune of others as a sign of our own inadequacy or deprivation. The Great Ball of Merit is a healthy corrective to envy. It brings us home, with a vast sense of ease, to our capacity for mutual enjoyment.

The practice takes two forms. The one closer to the ancient Buddhist meditation is this:

> Relax and close your eyes, relax into your breathing. Open your awareness to the fellow beings who share with you this planet-time .
> . .in this room . . . this neighborhood . . . this town . . . open to all those in this country . . . and in other lands . . . let your awareness encompass all beings living now in your world. Opening now to all time as well, let your awareness encompass all beings who ever lived .
> . . of all races and creeds and walks of life, rich, poor, kings and beggars, saints and sinners . . . like successive mountain ranges, the vast vistas of these fellow beings present themselves to your mind's eye . .
> . Now open yourself to the knowledge that in each of these innumerable lives some act of merit was performed. No matter how stunted or deprived the life, there was a gesture of generosity, a gift of love, an act of valor or self-sacrifice . . .on the battlefield or

workplace, hospital or home . . . from each of these beings in their endless multitudes arose actions of courage, kindness, of teaching and healing. Let yourself see these manifold and immeasurable acts of merit . . . as they arise in the vistas of your inner eye, sweep them together . . . sweep them into a pile in front of you . . . use your hands . . . pile them into a heap . . . pat them into a ball. It is the Great Ball of Merit . . . hold it and weigh it in your hands . . . rejoice in it, knowing that no act of goodness is ever lost. It remains ever and always a present resource . . . a resource for the transformation of life . . . and now, with jubilation and gratitude, you turn that great ball . . . turn it over . . . over . . .into the healing of our world.

As we can learn from modern science and picture in the holographic model of reality, our lives interpenetrate. In the fluid tapestry of space-time, there is at root no distinction between self and other. The acts and intentions of others are like seeds that can germinate and bear fruit through our own lives, as we take them into awareness and dedicate, or "turn over," that awareness to our empowerment. Thoreau, Gandhi, Martin Luther King, Dorothy Day, and the nameless heroes and heroines of our own day, all can be part of our Ball of Merit, on which we can draw for inspiration and endurance. Other traditions feature notions similar to this, such as the "cloud of witnesses" of which St. Paul spoke, or the Treasury or Merit in the Catholic Church.

The second, more workaday, version of the Ball of Merit meditation helps us open to the powers of others. It is in direct contrast to the commonly accepted, patriarchal notion of power as something personally owned and exerted over others. The exercise prepares us to bring expectant attention to our encounters with other beings, to view them with fresh openness and curiosity as to how they can enhance our Ball of Merit. We can play this inner game with someone opposite us on the bus or across the bargaining table. It is especially useful when dealing with a person with whom we may be in conflict.

What does this person add to my Great Ball of Merit? What gifts of intellect can enrich our common store? What reserves of stubborn endurance can she or he offer? What flights of fancy or powers of love lurk behind those eyes? What kindness or courage hides in those lips, what healing in those hands?

Then, as with the breathing-through exercise, we open ourselves to the presence of these strengths, inhaling our awareness of them. As our awareness grows, we experience our gratitude for them and our capacity to enhance and partake . . .

Often we let our perceptions of the powers of others make us feel inadequate. Alongside an eloquent colleague, we can feel inarticulate; in the presence of an athlete we can feel weak and clumsy. In the process, we can come to resent both ourself and the other person. In the light of the Great Ball of Merit, however, the gifts and good fortunes of others appear not as judgments, put-downs or competing challenges, but as resources we can honor and take pleasure in. We can learn to play detective, spying out treasures for the enhancement of life from even the unlikeliest material. Like air and sun and water, they form part of our common good.

In addition to releasing us from the mental cramp of envy, this spiritual practice—or game—offers two other rewards. One is pleasure in our own acuity, as our merit-detecting ability improves. The second is the response of others, who—while totally ignorant of the game we are playing—sense something in our manner that invites them to move more openly into the person they can be.

LEARNING TO SEE EACH OTHER

This exercise is derived from the Buddhist practice of the Brahmaviharas; it is known as the Four Abodes of the Buddha, which are lovingkindness, compassion, joy in the joy of others, and equanimity. Adapted for use in a social context, it helps us to see each other more truly and experience the depths of our interconnections.

In workshops, I offer this as a guided meditation, with participants sitting in pairs, facing each other. At its close, I encourage them to proceed to use it, or any portion they like, as they go about the business of their daily lives. It is an excellent antidote to boredom, when our eye falls on another person, say on the subway. It charges that idle movement with beauty and discovery. It also is useful when dealing with people whom we are tempted to dislike or disregard; it breaks open our accustomed ways of viewing them. When used like this, as a meditation-in-action, one does not, or course, gaze long and deeply into the other's eyes, as in the guided exercise. A seemingly casual glance is enough. The guided, group form goes like this:

Sit in pairs. Face each other. Stay silent. Take a couple of deep breaths, centering yourself and exhaling tension. Look into each other's eyes. If you feel discomfort or an urge to laugh or look away, just note that embarrassment with patience and gentleness toward yourself and come back, when you can, to your partner's eyes. You may never see this person again: the opportunity to behold the uniqueness of this particular human being is given to you now.

As you look into this being's eyes, let yourself become aware of the powers that are there . . . open yourself to awareness of the gifts and strengths and the potentialities in this being . . . Behind those eyes are unmeasured reserves of ingenuity and endurance, wit and wisdom. There are gifts there, of which this person her/himself is unaware. Consider what these untapped powers can do for the healing of our planet and the relishing of our common life . . . As you consider that, let yourself become aware of your desire that this person be free from fear. Let yourself experience how much you want this being to be free from anger . . . and free from greed . . . and free from sorrow . . . and the causes of suffering. Know that what you are now experiencing is the great lovingkindness. It is good for building a world.

Now, as you look into those eyes, let yourself become aware of the pain that is there. There are sorrows accumulated in that life's journey . . . There are failures and losses, griefs and disappointments beyond the telling. Let yourself open to them, open to that pain . . . to hurts that this person may never have shared with another being.

What you are now experiencing is the great compassion. It is good for the healing of our world.

As you look into those eyes, open to the thought of how good it would be to make common cause . . . consider how ready you might be to work together . . . to take risks in a joint venture . . . imagine the zest of that, the excitement and laughter of engaging together on a common project . . . acting boldly and trusting each other. As you open to that possibility, what you open to is the great wealth: the pleasure in each other's powers, the joy in each other's joy.

Lastly, let your awareness drop deep, deep within you like a stone, sinking below the level of what words or acts can express . . . breathe deeply and quietly . . . open your consciousness to the deep web of relationship that underlies and interweaves all experience, all knowing. It is the web of life in which you have taken being and in which you are supported. Out of that vast web you cannot fall . . . no stupidity or failure, no personal inadequacy, can ever sever you from that living web. For that is what you are . . . and what has brought you into being . . . feel the assurance of that knowledge. Feel the great peace . . . rest in it. Out of that great peace, we can venture everything. We can trust. We can act.

In doing this exercise we realize that we do not have to be particularly noble or saintlike in order to wake up to the power of our oneness with other beings. In our time, that simple awakening is the gift the bomb holds for us.

For all its horror and stupidity, the Bomb is also the manifestation of an awesome spiritual truth—the truth about the hell we create for ourselves when we cease to learn how to love. Saints, mystics, and prophets throughout the ages saw that law; now all can see it and none can escape its consequences. So we are caught now in a narrow place where we realize that Moses, Lao-Tzu, the Buddha, Jesus, and our own inner hearts were right all along; and we are as scared and frantic as cornered rats, and as dangerous. But the Bomb, if we let it, can turn that narrow cul-de-sac into a birth canal, pressing and pushing us through the dark pain of it, until we are delivered into . . . what? Love seems too weak a word. It is, as St. Paul said, "the glory that shall be revealed in us." It stirs in us now.

For us to regard the Bomb (or the dying seas, the poisoned air) as a monstrous injustice to us would suggest that we never took seriously the injunction to love. Perhaps we thought all along that Gautama and Jesus were kidding, or their teachings meant only for saints. But now we see, as an awful revelation, that we are all called to be saints—not good, necessarily, or pious or devout—but saints in the sense of just loving each other. One wonders what terrors this knowledge must hold that we fight it so, and flee from it in such pain. Can it be that the Bomb, by which we can extinguish all life, can tell us this? Can force us to face the terrors of love? Can be the occasion for our births?

It is in that possibility that we can take heart. Even in confusion and fear, with all our fatigues and petty faults, we can let that awareness work in and through our lives. Such simple exercises as those offered here can help us do that, and to begin to see ourselves and each other with fresh eyes.

Let me close with the same suggestion that closes our workshops. It is a practice that is corollary to the earlier death meditation, where we recognize that the person we meet may die in a nuclear war. Look at the next person you see. It may be lover, child, co-worker, postman, or your own face in the mirror. Regard him or her with the recognition that:

This person before me may be instrumental in saving us from nuclear war. In this person are gifts for the healing of our planet. In him/her are powers that can resound to the joy of all beings.

About the Contributors

Contributors

ROBERT AITKEN, head of the Diamond Sangha in Hawaii and co-founder of the Buddhist Peace Fellowship, is author of *The Mind of Clover, Taking the Path of Zen,* and *A Zen Wave.*

CHAGDUD TULKU, a Tibetan Buddhist lama, is the founder and president of the Mahakaruna Foundation, in Oregon. He is a meditation teacher, an artist, and a Tibetan doctor.

FRED EPPSTEINER, director of an outpatient mental health clinic in Florida, is editor of *Interbeing: Commentaries on the Tiep Hien Precepts,* by Thich Nhat Hanh.

CHRISTINA FELDMAN is a teacher of Vipassana meditation based at Gaia House in Devon, England. Tapes of her lectures are available through the Dharma Seed Tape Library.

NELSON FOSTER. a teacher at the Diamond Sangha in Hawaii and co-founder of the Buddhist Peace Fellowship, is editor of *The Wheel of Power: Buddhist Approaches to Politics* (forthcoming).

MAHA GHOSANANDA is head of the Khmer Buddhist Society of New England, working tirelessly to help Cambodian refugees. He is a Pali scholar and one of the few monks to survive the Pol Pot regime.

TENZIN GYATSO, THE XIVth DALAI LAMA is the spiritual leader of Tibetans worldwide and the head of the Tibetan government-in-exile. His books include *My Land and My People; Kindness, Clarity, and Insight;* and *Opening the Eye of New Awareness.*

KEN JONES, author of *The Social Face of Buddhism, Buddhism and Social Action,* and *Buddhism and the Bombs,* lives in Wales.

JACK KORNFIELD was co-founder of the Insight Meditation Society in Massachusetts, and is helping found Insight Meditation West in northern California. He is co-author (with Joseph Goldstein) of *Seeking the Heart of Wisdom: The Path of Insight Meditation,* and author of *Living Buddhist Masters.*

KENNETH KRAFT is assistant professor of Japanese Studies at the University of Pennsylvania and editor of *Zen: Tradition and Transition.*

JOANNA MACY teaches at the California Institute for Integral Studies and is author of *Dharma and Development* and *Despair and Personal Power in the Nuclear Age.* She is writing a book on the social teachings of the Buddha.

RAFE MARTIN, writer and storyteller, is author of *The Hungry Tigress and Other Traditional Asian Tales* and *Foolish Rabbit's Big Mistake.*

THICH NHAT HANH was founder of the School of Youth for Social Service in Vietnam, and chairman of the Vietnamese Buddhist Peace Delegation in Paris during the war. He lives in exile in France. His books include *Being Peace, Vietnam: Lotus in a Sea of Fire,* and *The Miracle of Mindfulness.*

CAO NGOC PHUONG is coordinator of a worldwide network of social workers helping Vietnamese refugees. The video documentary, *The Awakening Bell,* is about her work.

JUDITH RAGIR is an accupuncturist and a Zen student in Minnesota.

WALPOLA RAHULA is a Sri Lankan Buddhist monk and scholar. He is author of *What the Buddha Taught* and *The Heritage of the Bhikkhu*.

SULAK SIVARAKSA is Chair of the Asian Cultural Forum on Development and Director of the Pridi Banomyong Institute in Bangkok. He is author of *Religion and Development, A Buddhist Vision for Renewing Society*, and *Siamese Resurgence*. He has been a visiting Professor at Berkeley, Hawaii, and Toronto.

GARY SNYDER is a Pulitzer Prize-winning poet who lives in northern California. He is founder of the Ring of Bone Zendo, and author of *Axe Handles, Turtle Island, Earth House Hold*, and many other books.

CHARLENE SPRETNAK is author of *The Spiritual Dimension of Green Politics, Green Politics: The Global Promise* (with Fritjof Capra), *Lost Goddesses of Early Greece*, and is editor of *The Politics of Women's Spirituality*. She practices Vipassana meditation.

ROBERT A. F. THURMAN, co-founder of the American Institute of Buddhist Studies, is professor of Religion at Amherst College. He is translator of *The Holy Teachings of Vimalakirti* and author of *The Politics of Compassion* (forthcoming).

CHRISTOPHER TITMUSS, a teacher of vipassana meditation based at Gaia House in Devon, England, stood for British Parliament as a Green Party candidate in 1987. He is author of a forthcoming book of interviews with spiritual activists.

The Buddhist Peace Fellowship

STATEMENT OF PURPOSE

To make clear public witness to the Buddha Way as a way of peace and protection for all beings; to raise peace and ecology concerns among American Buddhists and to promote projects through which the Sangha may respond to these concerns; to encourage the delineation in English of the Buddhist way of nonviolence, building from the rich resources of traditional Buddhist teachings a foundation for new action; to offer avenues to realize the kinship among groups and members of the American and world Sangha; to serve as liaison to, and enlist support for, existing national and international Buddhist peace and ecology programs; to provide a focus for concerns over the persecution of Buddhists, as a particular expression of our intent to protect all beings; and to bring the Buddhist perspective to contemporary peace and ecology movements.

The Buddhist Peace Fellowship was founded in 1978, as a network of individuals and chapters. We are pleased to present *The Path of Compassion* as the first in a series of books on "engaged Buddhism." For information about membership, newsletter subscriptions, chapters, or general information, please write to Buddhist Peace Fellowship, P.O. Box 4650, Berkeley, CA 94704.